The Internet

Look for these and other books in the Lucent Overview Series:

Advertising
Censorship
Democracy
Elections
Hate Groups
Illiteracy
Schools

The Internet

by Harry Henderson

LUCENT BOOKS

LUCENT Overview Series

PINE HILL MIDDLE SCHOOL
LIBRARY

*To the real people
who are building virtual worlds*

Library of Congress Cataloging-in-Publication Data

Henderson, Harry, 1951–
    The Internet / by Harry Henderson.
       p. cm. — (Lucent overview series)
    Includes bibliographical references and index.
    Summary: Surveys the development of the Internet and includes an explanation of what it is, how it can be used, and what it means for the future.
    ISBN 1-56006-215-0 (alk. paper)
    1. Internet (Computer network)—Juvenile literature.
[1. Internet (Computer network)]   I. Title. II. Series.
    TK5105.875.I57H4596   1998
    004.67'8—dc21   97-39314
                                                                                 CIP
                                                                                  AC

No part of this book may be reproduced or used in any form or by any means, electrical, mechanical, or otherwise, including, but not limited to, photocopy, recording, or any information storage and retrieval system, without prior written permission from the publisher.

Copyright © 1998 by Lucent Books, Inc.
P.O. Box 289011, San Diego, CA 92198-9011
Printed in the U.S.A.

Contents

INTRODUCTION	6
CHAPTER ONE What Is the Internet?	10
CHAPTER TWO The World Is Your Classroom	24
CHAPTER THREE Business on the Net	35
CHAPTER FOUR The Electronic Marketplace	42
CHAPTER FIVE Information in the On-Line Age	54
CHAPTER SIX Virtual Communities	61
EPILOGUE A Challenging Future	73
NOTES	77
GLOSSARY	80
ORGANIZATIONS TO CONTACT	84
SUGGESTIONS FOR FURTHER READING	86
ADDITIONAL WORKS CONSULTED	89
INDEX	91
PICTURE CREDITS	96
ABOUT THE AUTHOR	96

Introduction

THE MICROCOMPUTER REVOLUTION of the 1980s brought personal computers to desktops, kitchen tables, and classrooms. The clatter of typewriters was replaced by the click of computer keyboards. Computer terminals drove card catalogs out of libraries. Pinball parlors became video arcades. Encyclopedias that used to sell for $1,200 could be bought for $50 on compact disc. Students began to include color graphics in their reports. Many elementary and high school students started to program computers and use software, such as word processing programs and spreadsheets.

Although most people were not yet aware of it, another computer revolution began during that same decade. Computers were being hooked together into networks. Electronic mail (often called e-mail for short), bulletin boards, and on-line services such as America Online, Prodigy, and CompuServe began to change the way people communicated with one another.

Meanwhile, a number of knowledgeable students and researchers at universities and corporations were using a growing web of connected computer networks that became known as the Internet (or just "the Net"). In the early 1990s, new software called the World Wide Web made the Internet much easier for nontechnical people to use.

The on-line explosion

By the mid-1990s, usage of the Internet was exploding. According to an estimate by a company called Network

Wizards, the number of "hosts" offering their ideas or services on the Net had risen from about 5 million in January 1995 to over 16 million in January 1997. This number seems to be doubling every year and is likely to reach 100 million by the end of the century. Estimates of the actual number of people who connect to the Net and use it regularly vary between 30 and 40 million in the United States, plus a growing number worldwide.

As the popularity of the Internet soared, the media began to feature it in news stories. Political leaders proposed programs to connect all American schools to the Net, rules to regulate business on the Net, restrictions on the use of encryption (coded messages), and laws to keep sexual or violent images off the computer screens of young people. Meanwhile, businesses ranging from local pizza parlors to

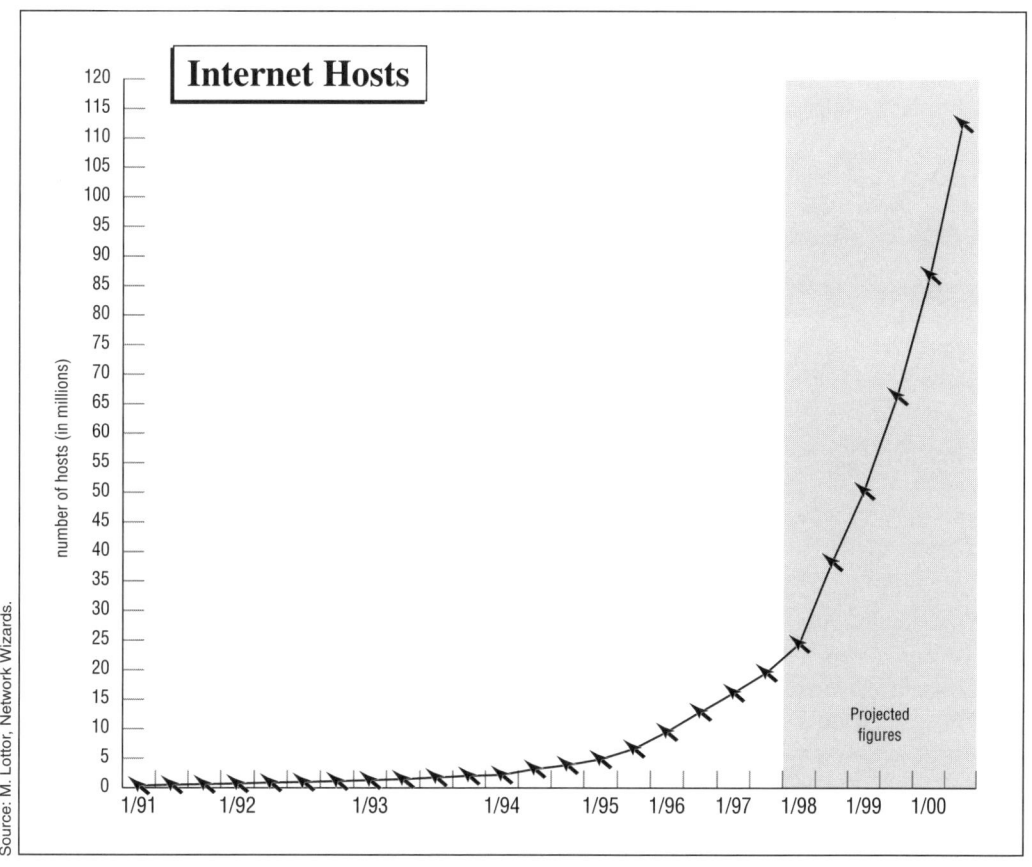

nationwide bookstore chains began to put their menus, catalogs, and advertising on the Net. Internet and electronic mail addresses became a routine part of ads, brochures, and letterheads.

Tools, opportunities, and challenges

Today, as the Internet and related technologies begin to take an important place in many people's daily lives, people and institutions are struggling to define how these tools should be used.

A tool is not good or evil in itself. A car, for example, can be used to drive to a picnic spot in the country. It can also be used by bank robbers to escape the police. A telephone can be used to call 911 for help, to chat with a friend, or to swindle people with "get rich quick" schemes.

In the same way, computers and networks are being used to help people learn, share ideas, enjoy games, and run businesses. They are also sometimes used to carry messages of hate, violence, or raw sex. On-line advertising "pitches," like their traditional counterparts, can give consumers interesting new choices, but they can also be used to mislead or swindle them.

Like all technology, computers and networks are "amplifiers" that give both the good citizen and the criminal

Political leaders have proposed laws that would restrict material posted on the Net to prevent children from being exposed to violent and sexually explicit images.

the power to do more, with greater speed and involving more people. It is often not clear how we can protect people from criminal activity while respecting liberty and privacy. The very freedom and flexibility that make the Internet useful in so many ways also make it difficult to prevent abuses.

Even when new technologies are used for good purposes, they may have unexpected side effects. The automobile changed the way people relate to the physical environment and brought problems of pollution, congestion, and the depletion of resources. Computer networks are changing the way people relate to their *social* environment. On the one hand, they have brought new freedom for many people to work where, when, and how they want. A look at the classified Help Wanted section of any newspaper reveals dozens of job categories such as "Java programmer" or "webmaster" that did not even exist before the 1990s. On the other hand, human contact and face-to-face relationships may be giving way to a more artificial world of text screens and mail messages. And if everyone can be anywhere, what happens to people's roots and ties to their community?

The new developments surveyed in this book will bring exciting opportunities to today's students. They will also raise questions about what it means to be human and to relate to other people. By the time the young readers of this book have graduated and begun their careers, today's computer networks will seem as primitive as an old black-and-white TV set does today. But the opportunities, challenges, and questions will remain.

1

What Is the Internet?

THE INTERNET DID not spring up overnight. It has roots that go back almost as far as computing itself. The first computers were built in the 1940s, just after World War II. The early machines, such as ENIAC, were huge, expensive, and rather fragile because they used bulky vacuum tubes to perform calculations and store numbers. Because these computers were so large and expensive, only a few large corporations and government agencies used them.

By the 1950s, the Cold War between the United States and the Soviet Union was under way. Military planners had to deal with a world where nuclear-armed bombers and missiles might attack with little warning. They began to use computers such as a giant machine called SAGE to coordinate radar sightings and plan counterattacks.

In the 1950s, a "think tank" called the RAND Corporation concluded that in any future war, many of the main centers of communications—telephone switching offices, broadcast stations, military and government buildings—would quickly be destroyed. How could government and military leaders continue to issue orders to whatever forces were left? RAND researcher Paul Baran suggested a solution "that messages be broken into units of equal size and that the network route these message units along a functioning path to their destination where they would be reassembled into coherent wholes."[1] If there was any path left to the destination, even an indirect one, the network would find it and the message would get through.

In the 1960s, the Defense Department's Advanced Research Projects Agency (ARPA) began to design such a network, which became known as ARPAnet. In 1970 the network began with connections between four western universities: Stanford; University of California, Los Angeles; University of California, San Diego; and the University of Utah.

The ARPAnet turned out to be quite different from what the early planners had imagined, however. The planners had thought the network would use very large mainframe computers. Its purpose was to process large amounts of data, such as radar readings and firing commands. They did not think in terms of people using the network to communicate directly with one another.

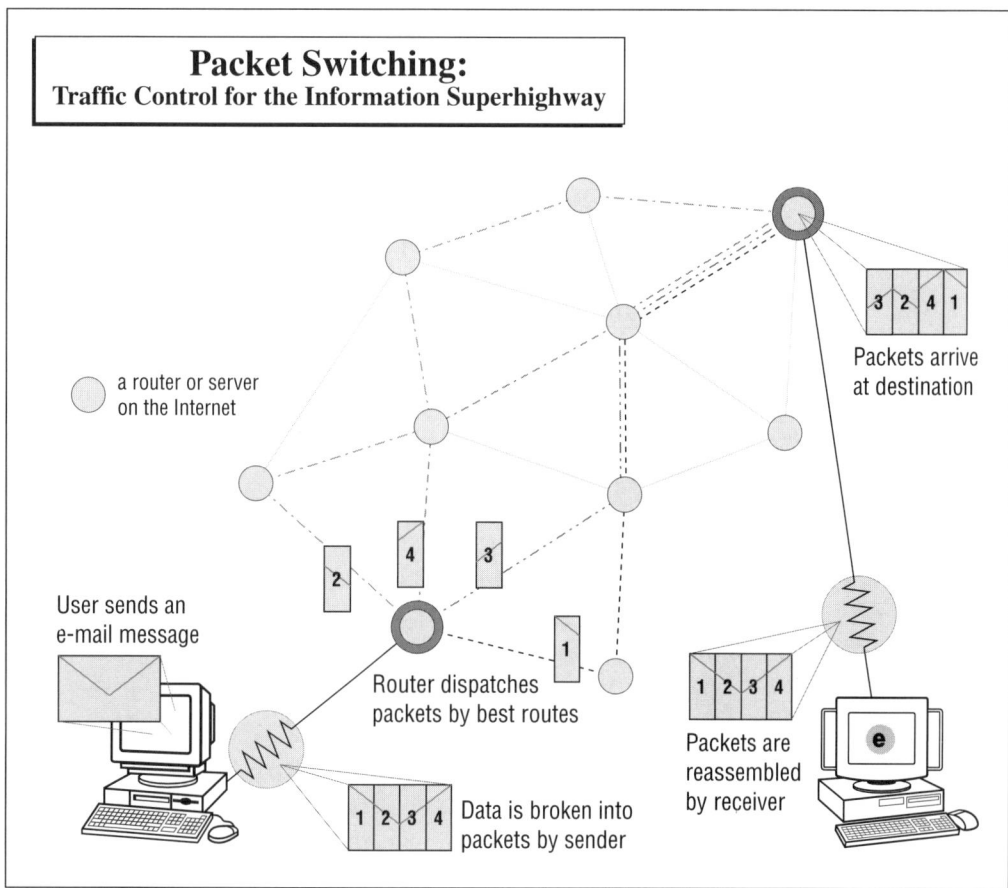

Packet Switching:
Traffic Control for the Information Superhighway

- a router or server on the Internet
- User sends an e-mail message
- Router dispatches packets by best routes
- Data is broken into packets by sender
- Packets arrive at destination
- Packets are reassembled by receiver

The Ferranti Pegasus computer (pictured) was considered a medium-size, multipurpose computer in 1950.

In the late 1950s, however, designers started building a new kind of computer. Computers such as Digital Equipment's TX series were not room-size mainframes, but merely the size of a refrigerator. These "minicomputers" were still very expensive by modern standards, but major universities could install them for use by their researchers and students.

Minicomputers were not only smaller than mainframes, they were used differently. Mainframes used "batch processing," in which a program and data on punched cards were given to an operator, who ran the program and returned the results, often hours to days later. But minicomputer designers hooked their new machines up to a typewriter-like terminal at which commands could be input directly by programmers and users without needing punched cards. Unlike batch processing, the computer could print out results immediately or display them on a video screen.

Around the same time, researchers designed the first time-sharing operating systems. Instead of running only one program at a time, the time-sharing system let the computer switch from one task to another, doing some work on the first one, then some on the second, and so on. This meant that many users could be hooked up to the same computer, sharing its resources. Because the computer "thinks" faster than people, it was as though each person had his or her own computer. This brought the cost of computing per user way down.

Once many users were connected to computers, it was inevitable that they would want to talk to one another. The person in charge of the computer (the "system administrator") needed to keep users informed about when the computer would be available. A beginning user might want to ask a more experienced user for help. People working together on the same project needed to coordinate their efforts. Since they were all connected to the same computer, why not use it as a kind of bulletin board for the community? By 1972 users on the ARPAnet were exchanging electronic mail messages and using a program called FTP (File Transfer Protocol) to transfer files back and forth between computers.

In addition to ARPAnet, a variety of other networks for researchers and students began to spring up. Unfortunately, these networks all used different protocols, or procedures for sending and receiving messages. In order to link the networks—to create an "internet"— there would have to be a common protocol. In 1974 researchers Vinton Cerf and Robert Kahn released the Internet Protocol (IP) and Transmission Control Protocol (TCP), which together would be used for the Internet. The main idea of TCP/IP was that data packets or "datagrams" would have headers (like the address on an envelope) specifying where they came from and their intended destination. The routing computers would have tables showing the available computer connections, just as a mail sorter in a post office might have a list of zip codes. The router would select the best connection and send the packet along. If it did not receive acknowledgment that the packet had been received, the router would send it again or, if necessary, try an alternate route.

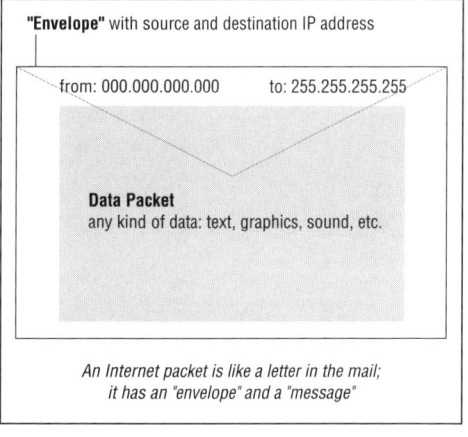

An Internet packet is like a letter in the mail; it has an "envelope" and a "message"

As Internet historians Katie Hafner and Matthew Lyon put it:

> The new scheme worked in much the same way that shipping containers are used to transfer goods. The boxes have a standard size and shape. They can be filled with anything from televisions to underwear to automobiles—content doesn't matter. They move by ship, rail, or truck.... The only thing necessary to ensure cross-compatibility [ability to work with different systems] is the specialized equipment used to transfer the containers from one mode of transport to the next. The cargo itself doesn't leave the container until it reaches its destination.[2]

Just as the parts for a large machine could be shipped in a variety of containers and be uncrated and assembled at the destination, a computer file such as an e-mail message, a news posting, or a graphics image is broken into packets by the transport program, sent by the routing system, and reassembled by software at the destination computer. Other than for speed, it does not matter exactly how the packets get there—by regular phone lines, fiber-optic cables, or radio links. By 1983 TCP/IP was in place, and the Internet was born.

Weaving the World Wide Web

By the 1980s, many new on-line services had become available. Users of Unix, a popular and very versatile computer operating system used on many college campuses, had designed tools that let users not only send electronic mail, but "chat" in real time and post messages in a variety of topical forums called newsgroups. Meanwhile, users of personal computers could choose from several on-line services that were fairly easy to use.

In 1989 Tim Berners-Lee—a researcher at CERN, a big European physics laboratory—was struggling to coordinate the many groups of scientists who worked there. The Internet was available, of course, and so were electronic mail and newsgroups. The problem was that everything someone might want to do on the Internet required that users learn to operate a separate program: one for mail, one for news, one for file transfer, several different programs for accessing databases, and so on.

Berners-Lee had worked with hypertext, a system that is used in many on-line encyclopedias and educational programs today. In a hypertext encyclopedia, an article on French history might give a general summary in which a number of key words such as **Napoleon** appear underlined or in a different color. The reader who wants to learn more about Napoleon clicks on that "link" and is shown, perhaps, a biography of that leader. The biography, in turn, mentions Napoleon's role in the **French Revolution**, and those words are also highlighted, ready to be explored with a mouse click. Thus with hypertext, a reader can quickly explore related concepts and get background information to improve understanding of a topic.

Berners-Lee decided to use a hypertext system to link together all the different kinds of information available on the Internet. Berners-Lee created a software package called the World Wide Web. The Web consisted of an ever-growing collection of pages of information. Each page had highlighted links that would take the reader to additional or related information. For example, a university might have a page that gives the names of its departments, such as Computer Science, English, and Music. The department names would be highlighted, and clicking on one with the mouse would bring up a page with more information about that department. In turn, the department page might point to individual pages giving information about each professor in the department, and so on.

Tim Berners-Lee spent more than a decade developing the World Wide Web.

Interest soars

In order for all this to work, each page had a unique "address" that would tell the software where to find it. A system called HTTP (Hypertext Transmission Protocol) passes requests for pages to the computers that maintain them. On each page, a special language called HTML (Hypertext Markup Language) specifies how software on the user's computer will show different parts of the page, such as headers, text fonts, lists or tables of information, and so on.

Of course at the time Berners-Lee started the World Wide Web, there was not very much information that was already provided in hypertext form. There were, however, plenty of databases, menus (using a system called Gopher), and other services that people could access. Berners-Lee could get the Web off to a running start by creating links to the programs that provided access to existing databases and other services.

At first, the World Wide Web showed only text, not pictures. But in 1993 researchers at the National Center for Supercomputing Applications (NCSA) released a program called Mosaic. Mosaic included "plug-in" utility programs that could show pictures, animations, and even video as well as play music and recorded voices. Once people saw Mosaic, interest in the Internet among ordinary computer users soared.

Who is on the Internet?

A person or organization that wants to be on the Net begins by creating a home page. In a way, a home page is part business card, part advertisement, and part table of contents.

Home pages for government agencies, nonprofit organizations, and educational institutions usually describe the purpose of the organization and provide links to particular departments or services, as well as news bulletins. For example, a consumer protection agency might include bulletins about dangerous products.

Businesses can use their web pages for several purposes. A software company, for example, might have descriptions of its products. There is also likely to be technical support—help for users who have problems understanding how to use the products or who have encountered bugs in the software. There may also be listings of available jobs. Other kinds of businesses use their web pages as an advertising and sales tool.

Many individuals have their own web pages. Originally, creating a web page meant creating the hypertext by embedding HTML commands by hand. Recently, however, a number of software packages have made putting together web pages no more difficult than using a word processor.

A University of Kansas fan updates a website dedicated to the Jayhawks basketball team. Software packages have simplified the creation and maintenance of sites like this one.

An individual web page is limited only by its creator's imagination. Many pages have photos of family members, lists of favorite music or hobbies, and links to the creator's favorite websites. These pages can become very elaborate, however. A person interested in baseball, for example, could provide links to hundreds of baseball-related sites, links to live updates of games in progress, fantasy baseball leagues, and so on.

Getting connected

How does a person get access to the Internet and the World Wide Web? A growing number of elementary and high school students are getting connected to the Internet at school. Most universities already provide access for their students. People whose careers involve computers (programmers, engineers, scientists, researchers, and so on) are likely to have Internet connections at their workplace.

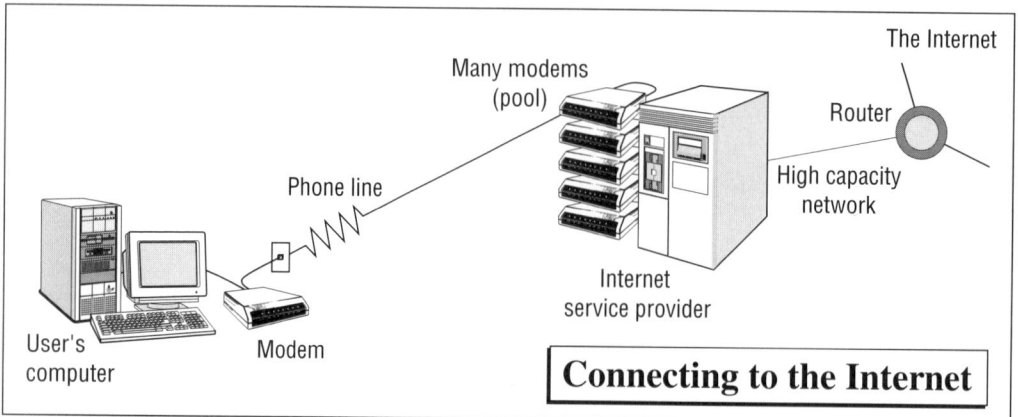

Connecting to the Internet

Finally, anyone can connect to the Internet from their home by buying a personal computer and a modem (a device that connects computers to phone lines) and getting an account from an Internet service provider (ISP), usually for a monthly fee of around $20. Alternatively, the user can join an information service such as America Online, which provides added features.

However one gets access, connecting to the Net begins by having one's personal computer or terminal make a connection to a computer called a server. This connection can be made over a regular telephone, a special high-speed telephone line, or a direct connection that is part of a "local area network" found in many organizations. Before a connection is accepted, the user must provide a user ID and a password.

Once connected, the user generally runs a program called a web browser. This program serves as a kind of window into the ever-changing world of the Internet. Popular browsers include Netscape Navigator and Microsoft Internet Explorer.

Surfing and searching

Most web browsers begin by presenting a "start page" to the user. The start page typically gives some tips for browsing and searching, plus links to lists of recommended websites in categories such as entertainment, business, education, and technology. The user begins to learn his or her way around the Web by clicking on these links and exploring different kinds of information and services. Because it is like riding wherever the waves might lead, this kind of Web use is often called "surfing the Net." The browser also lets users "bookmark" the site currently being displayed so that it is easy to return to it at a later time.

After a session or two, users may want to explore the Web more systematically. Sites such as Yahoo! have created a kind of subject catalog to the Web. Usually the catalog begins with a list of broad topics, such as science, politics, sports, entertainment, business, and technical. Clicking on one of these categories displays a list of subcategories. For example, the entertainment category might include actors and actresses, movies, TV shows, musical groups, and so on. Clicking on one of these subtopics gets a list of recommended websites to explore.

Search engines

There is a third way to find things on the Web. Suppose a student wants to do a class report on how people are seeking to protect their privacy in the computer age. The student can turn to a "search engine" such as Alta Vista and tell it to find all pages that include keywords or phrases such as "privacy protection." Unlike a catalog site, a search engine automatically scans the entire Web and creates a continually updated keyword index of all the pages it can find. When a search phrase is given to the search engine, it displays a list of all the sites that match one or more keywords. The list normally begins with the

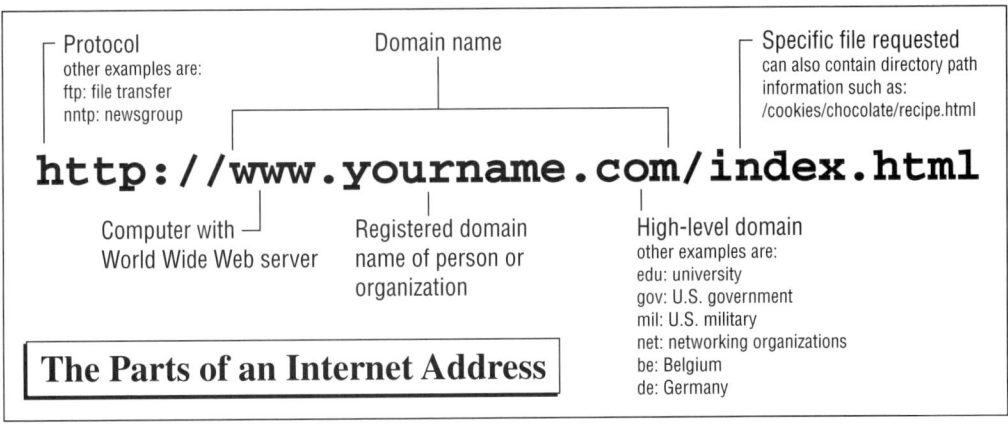

The Parts of an Internet Address

closest matches (matching all or most of the words) and proceeds to partial matches.

Each of the three ways of using the Web has its advantages and disadvantages. Surfing can be fun and can lead to surprising discoveries, but it is a hit-and-miss, time-consuming way to try to answer specific questions. A catalog site makes it easy to find recommended sites on a particular topic, but gives only a small proportion of what may be available. A search engine can find almost anything, but often retrieves a large number of "hits" that can be difficult to sort through. Part of learning to use the Web is learning when to use each technique.

Using the Web, therefore, requires good thinking and research skills. Just as students were once taught how to use a library card catalog, many schools are now teaching on-line searching skills.

Usenet newsgroups

The Internet offers a number of services that let users communicate with other individuals or with the world at large. One of the oldest (and most popular) services is called Usenet. A set of programs called Netnews lets users type messages (called articles) and "post" them so that

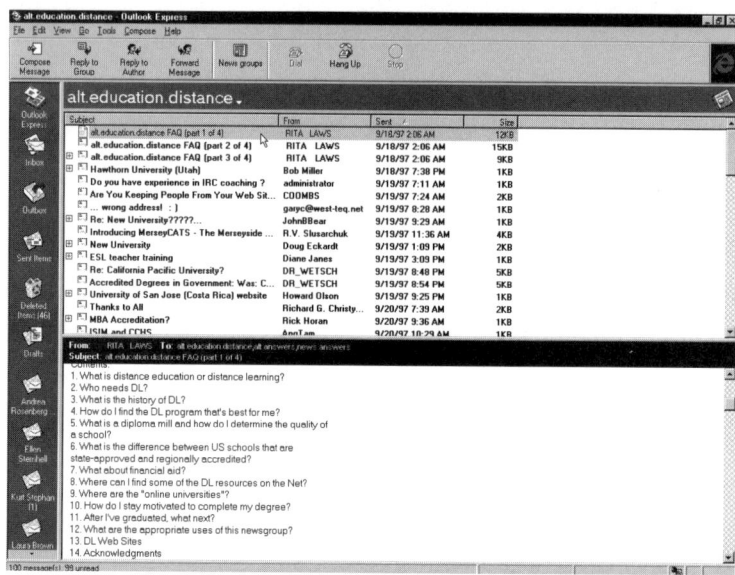

Usenet groups are organized by topic, listing articles posted by Internet users.

they are distributed to computers throughout the Internet. The messages are organized into topical newsgroups. There are now over ten thousand such groups, divided into several major categories including the following:

Category	Meaning
comp	computer hardware, software, operating systems
sci	science and technology
soc	social issues, politics
rec	recreation, sports, hobbies, arts
news	using the news system; proposals to add groups
misc	miscellaneous topics
talk	various discussion groups with many participants
alt	alternative versions of newsgroups, less formal

The name of a newsgroup is divided into parts, much like an Internet address. For example, a group called rec.sports.baseball.statistics belongs in the rec (recreation) category and the sports subcategory; the particular sport is baseball, and the aspect of baseball to be discussed is statistics (things like batting averages and home run totals).

Electronic mail

While Usenet is used for discussion groups, electronic mail enables individuals to send messages directly to one another. Whether using a school or business account, an individual ISP account, or membership in an on-line service, e-mail users now number in the tens of millions.

Until a few years ago, users connected to different networks or on-line services often had a hard time sending messages to one another because the message formats were

A simple electronic (e-mail) message is typed and then transmitted across the Internet.

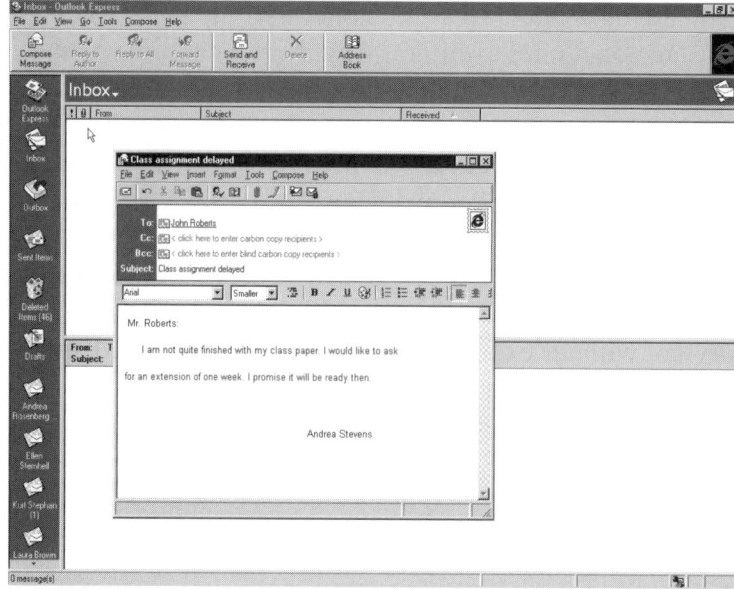

incompatible. Today, however, nearly all e-mail uses a simple addressing system similar to that used for web pages. For example, if a user named Maria Hernandez has an account with an Internet provider called Yournet, her e-mail address might be mhernandez@yournet.com. Notice that the person's user ID (used to log on to the system) comes first, then the @ symbol followed by the name of the "host" computer where she has an account. If Maria also has her own web page, it might have a web address like the following: www.yournet.com/users/mhernandez.htm.

E-mail is used for a wide variety of purposes. Within a school, students might use it to leave questions for teachers or even to turn in assignments. Several students working on a project together can send drafts of their work to one another for review. Businesses use e-mail for much of the communication that used to require phone calls or written memos. While browsing the Web, a user can often click on a "mail link" at a website and send the owner a comment or a request for more information.

A whole group of people can use e-mail to keep in touch. By using software that sets up a "mailing list," any member of the group can send a message that will be automatically distributed to everyone in the group. Mailing lists are sometimes used in a way similar to Usenet newsgroups, but with more privacy, because only people who have joined the mailing list can see the messages.

E-mail has some real advantages over traditional means of communication. People whose jobs involve frequent travel can send messages without having to play "telephone tag." An e-mail message can be sent from San Francisco to Tokyo at no added cost beyond that of the Internet service, without expensive long-distance charges. E-mail has largely replaced package shippers and even the fax machine as a way to move documents around the world.

E-mail does have some disadvantages. Problems with the network or a host computer can sometimes result in messages being "bounced" or returned to sender, or even disappearing without a trace. And because it is so easy to send e-mail automatically, electronic mailboxes can be filled with unwanted messages or advertising.

Informative and interactive

By providing news and mail services along with web pages, the Internet combines distribution of information with interactive communication. Internet users are not passive viewers as with television. They can respond to what they see and contribute to ongoing discussions.

By the middle of the twentieth century, the telephone had largely replaced letter writing for most personal communication. At the century's end, however, electronic mail may be bringing back the lost art of letter writing in a new, more streamlined form.

2

The World Is Your Classroom

SINCE THE 1980S, there has been much discussion about the need to make sure that today's elementary and high school students are "computer literate"—that is, able to understand how computers work and to use them in such applications as word processing, spreadsheet calculations, and databases. Both educators and business leaders are concerned that today's students may not be prepared for the kinds of jobs that will be available in the early twenty-first century. Increasingly, most of the better-paid jobs, whether in science and technology, finance, sales and marketing, or even manufacturing, will require good computer skills.

Computer skills are not just something to be used in a future career, however. Students are using computers and the Internet in today's schools to learn subjects such as social studies, mathematics, science, literature, and art in new ways. A *USA Today* poll in April 1997 revealed that 56 percent of American students have used the Internet in some way for a school project, and 77 percent of students say they prefer using the Internet to using books and magazines. A survey of teachers said that about 75 percent of teachers felt the Internet was an important educational tool, though many teachers said they did not see actual evidence that the Net helped students perform better.

Reference resources

The Internet gives students access to a vast reference library. Many Internet sites offer current stories from newspapers and magazines. Government agencies provide census data, weather forecasts, and information about which fields are likely to offer graduates the best employment opportunities. Other sites offer data about the growth of the economy or the latest findings in AIDS research.

There are Internet sites with library catalogs, pictures of items in museum collections, and collections of documents ranging from the *Federalist Papers* to the latest reports on global warming. The Net certainly provides many resources for homework and school projects.

Using the Internet to change the way people learn

It is a mistake to think of the Net as just a big library, however. The communications tools of the Net are also changing the *way* people learn. The Internet offers new opportunities for kids to learn by working together in the same way their parents do at work. Deneen Frazier's book *Internet for Kids* suggests a number of group learning projects, such as the following:

Three or more students with an Internet connection can create a news bureau that reports local stories and posts them on the Net. One student acts as editor in chief and decides which stories are worth pursuing. Another student serves as reporter and researches and writes the story. A third student is the copy editor, making sure the writing is complete, clear, and grammatical. In fact, there are already a number of news agencies for youth, such as one sponsored by the Global SchoolNet Foundation. These agencies provide guidelines and help for students who want to become regular news contributors. These students are learning more than computer skills: They are learning how workers with different jobs work together to make a business run.

Science students can also use the Net to do things that would have been difficult or impossible only a few years ago. By using e-mail to keep in touch with groups of students in other parts of the country (or in other countries), students can compare notes on weather and practice weather forecasting. NASA often provides special websites

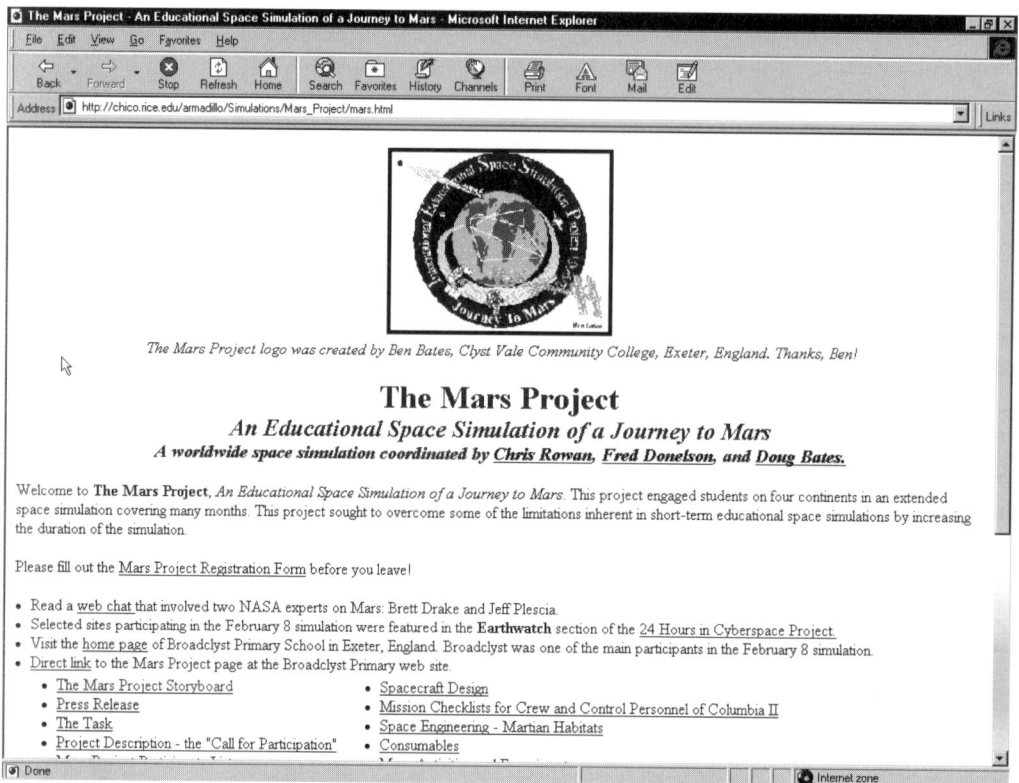

Cooperative learning sites such as the Mars Project can involve students in adventures they could previously only imagine. Students in the Mars Project become the simulated crew of a monthlong voyage to Mars.

that students can use to receive the latest findings from space probes such as the Mars *Pathfinder*. Ecology students can "adopt" an animal in the wild and track its daily activities. And in social studies, students can create polls, put them on a web page, and learn how other young people feel about important social issues.

The Internet gives students new opportunities to relate to people from other cultures who have very different living situations. For example, one networking project linked students in a one-room Eskimo school in the far north to students in Alberta, Canada; New York; Oregon; and Texas. The non-Eskimo students were asked, "What do we have in our classroom that you probably don't have in yours?" The answer turned out to be "a wood-burning stove." And while students have often written to foreign "pen pals" as a class project, e-mail and computer conferencing offer something much more like an ongoing conversation.

Such conversations can become quite thought provoking. A project called KIDLINK starts students with the following four questions:

1. Who am I?
2. What do I want to be when I grow up?
3. How do I want the world to be better when I grow up?
4. What can I do now to make this happen?[3]

A related program, KIDFORUM, has sponsored "virtual vacations," where students from Europe, Russia, Slovenia, and Tasmania can experience the daily life of their counterparts through the use of conferencing software.

The Internet has also been a benefit for students who are disabled or have other special needs. A blind eleventh grader named Randy Hammer was given the opportunity to join the DO-IT (Disabilities, Opportunities, Internetworking Technology) program at the University of Washington. According to Randy:

> Getting Internet access was the best thing that ever happened to me. In a way, my computer and access to the net has become my eyes to the world. I can read a newspaper [with the aid of a screen reading program], talk to people around the world, and get materials for class papers, unlike before when I had to depend on others to get the resources I needed.[4]

Who gets connected?

The possibilities for computers and the Internet in education are exciting, but there is a gap between what is possible and what is actually available to most of America's students. An organization called Computer Professionals for Social Responsibility (CPSR) declared in a 1993 statement that

> universal access to the NII [National Information Infrastructure, or "Information Superhighway"] is a necessary and basic condition of citizenship in our information-driven society. Guaranteeing such access is therefore an absolute requirement for any degree of equity [fairness].[5]

The group goes on to declare that all people should have affordable access to all features of the Net, with freedom of speech, protection of privacy, and use of technology that promotes fairness in the workplace.

But despite its many potential benefits, only about 20 percent of America's elementary and high school classrooms had Internet access by mid-1997. America's schools have about 50 million students and 3 million teachers. Getting them all connected to the Net is a daunting task.

On March 3, 1996, President Bill Clinton and Vice President Al Gore proclaimed NetDay '96, a cooperative effort of corporations, local businesspeople, school districts, parents, and children. The goal is to bring the Internet into as many of America's classrooms as possible. The results can be impressive. For example, a NetDay in Oakland, California, involved 500 volunteers wiring 300 rooms in 50 schools.

Clinton said that this effort was "an inspiration to the nation. In a way, NetDay is a modern version of an old-fashioned barn raising. . . . We are putting the future at the fingertips of your children and we are doing it in the best American tradition."[6]

There have been several more NetDays since then. But even with businesses donating computers and volunteers doing the wiring, using the Internet effectively is more than just a matter of hardware. Many teachers took their education courses at a time when computers were just starting to enter the schools. According to educator Damon Moore, "We're at an F in training. Most teachers have very little knowledge as to what's available online. They know about the Internet, but they've never seen or used it."[7]

In many classrooms, in fact, it's not the teacher who is the computer expert, as author Matt Carlson explains:

Vice President Al Gore and President Bill Clinton kick off NetDay '96 at Ygnacio Valley High School in Concord, California.

> During a recent visit to a high school computer club, I was introduced to Michael, a bright and outgoing sophomore. . . . As I talked to Michael, I learned that he had started programming in Basic and Pascal [computer languages] when he was nine. Now he was interested in C++ and object-oriented programming [more modern languages]. Michael told me that he had designed [Internet] home pages for several major corporations and worked on a contract basis for a local service

provider helping businesses getting on the Internet. Imagine a 15-year-old whose computer skills would meet and exceed more than 50% of [the requirements of] a given Sunday's data processing classified [ads].[8]

Students and teachers must often struggle together in schools where there are large class sizes, inadequate budgets, and social problems that end up being higher priorities than computerization. Students from suburban families often have their own computers at home as well as lavish equipment at school. In inner-city schools, however, students may only be able to use computers and the Internet a couple hours a month. And because they often lack reading skills, disadvantaged students may find mastering the on-line world to be very difficult.

Internet advocates like to say that "there is no race in cyberspace" since on-line communication does not reveal physical appearance or racial identity. But only about half as many African American households have access to a computer at home as white households do. This may be changing, however. Stafford L. Battle, an African American businessperson, is spreading the gospel of technology in the minority community. Battle recalls:

> At first, we would go to a library or church to speak, and there would only be three or four people there. Today, there are a lot more African Americans online. But there is still some technophobia. One African American gentleman . . . told me computers were a white man's thing. Until someone shows them how to use the technology to their benefit, it will be foreign to them.[9]

The Net and educational reform

The movement to get schools onto the Net may be linked with the larger struggle to reform the school system. By themselves, computers may not be able to overcome the problems that are making America's schools fall behind their foreign counterparts. As astronomer and Internet critic Clifford Stoll points out:

> To one person, computer literacy means that a student can type on a keyboard. Another sees it as the ability to use standard tools to send, copy, or delete files. A third expects stu-

dents to write a simple program in BASIC. One teacher showed me an exam where a student had to describe the functions of different pieces of hardware.

But what does computer literacy mean to a child who can't read at grade level and can't interpret what she reads? What does it mean to a teenager who can't write grammatically, not to mention analytically [using logic]? If a child doesn't have a questioning mind, what good does all this networked technology do?[10]

Herbert Kohl notes that schools often try to fit the new technology into the same old system:

> Many schools have been incorporating computers as they would new textbooks or laboratory equipment, or adding new classes to curriculum or new departments with specialists hired to teach new subject areas. The institutional structure of schooling remains unchanged. . . . Computers become an add-on. In computer labs, machines are lined up in a spare room and used for drill and practice in arithmetic and language arts, or as rewards for students who do their other work quickly and well.[11]

Some teachers may be tempted to use computers just to hold students' attention. Marilyn Durch, a high school English teacher, worries that

> computers are lollipops that rot your teeth. The kids love them. But once they get hooked, they get bored without all

the whoopee stuff. It makes reading a book seem tedious. Books don't have sound effects and [the students'] brains have to do all the work.[12]

This debate has happened before. Shortly after it became available in the late 1940s, television was touted as a wonderful educational tool. Soon, however, disappointed critics began to refer to the "vast wasteland" of meaningless programs being watched by a nation of "couch potatoes." Could the Internet turn out to be a similar disappointment?

Internet advocates, however, point out that computers and the Internet are interactive. Unlike television viewers, Internet viewers can pick and choose information in detail, rather than just changing channels. They can also engage in on-line conversations with other users. Certainly using the Internet involves skills that are an important part of education. Even more than TV, information technology challenges educators to rethink what education should really mean.

Virtual classrooms and lifelong learning

While educators struggle to bring more of the information age into the schoolroom, some innovators are getting rid of the schoolroom itself. Today a growing number of colleges offer "distance learning" courses. In distance learning, students do not sit together in a classroom or lecture hall. Instead, they receive video lectures from the professor and use e-mail or chat software for class discussions. The professor may live in New Haven, Connecticut, and the student in Tokyo. They never physically meet one another.

Management expert Peter Drucker believes that as the cost of attending a traditional college continues to soar, "universities won't survive. The future is outside the traditional campus, outside the traditional classroom. Distance learning is coming on fast."[13] Drucker may be right about the movement to distance learning. In 1993 *Peterson's*, the college guidebook, listed only 93 "cyberschools" that offered classes on-line. By 1997, however, the *Distance Learning* guide listed 762.

Some traditional educators respond by saying that a college education is more than a set of course credits. James Aisner of the Harvard Business School insists that "being together, talking to people in the dorms or residence halls, is an essential part of the learning process here."[14]

Nevertheless, a student attending the University of Phoenix may expect to pay about $100,000 for tuition, room, board, and other expenses for a four-year undergraduate degree. The university charges about $33,000 for the same degree through distance learning. While the distance learner pays more for each credit at most colleges, there are no on-campus living expenses.

Distance learning also lets older people who already have full-time jobs continue their education without giving up their work. Because information age jobs require constant retraining as technology advances, many experts tell today's young people to expect "a lifetime of learning." Indeed, many people seem to be returning to college later in life. In 1972 only 28 percent of U.S. college and university students were over twenty-five years old. In 1994 the proportion of older students had climbed to 41 percent. Future employees may find distance learning courses to be just what they need to keep up with a changing business world.

The Internet also offers opportunities for older people who have retired from the workplace. In 1997 the federal agency that runs Medicare announced a program that will put computers in hundreds of senior citizen centers throughout the country to help older Americans make better decisions about their health care. But the Net offers more than information: It can also provide a social outlet for people who must stay home because of age or disability.

Between graduation and retirement, workers in academic fields will use the Internet as a vital research tool. The more a field depends on timely access to an ever-growing stream of information, the more impact the Internet will have on how researchers do their work. Given the rapid pace of discoveries in fields such as genetics, medicine, space exploration, and computer science, it is not surprising that scientists are using the Net to help them keep up.

Scientists and researchers on the Net

The Net began changing scientific research even before it had much effect on education. Traditionally, scientists submit papers describing their research to scientific journals. The journals send copies of the papers to other respected scientists who are familiar with the field. The reviewers point out any problems they find with how the research has been done. The author of the paper can then revise it. While some news spreads by word of mouth, it might take many months before a scientific breakthrough becomes known to most scientists and to the general public.

Today papers are still reviewed before they are officially published. But many researchers release draft copies of their papers on the Net, where they can get quick feedback. Word of discoveries gets out faster. The pace of science speeds up, and sometimes scientists in different parts of the world can discover they are working on similar ideas and combine their efforts.

Using the Net to spread science news can have unfortunate effects, however. When G. Stanley Pons of the University of

The Internet can serve as a social outlet for those confined to their homes because of age or disability.

Utah and Professor Martin Fleischmann of Great Britain's Southhampton University claimed to have produced cold nuclear fusion (a possible source of safe, portable, inexpensive power), many readers on the Net and in the media did not realize that these claims had not gone through the scientific review process. It turned out that the experiments could not be reproduced in other laboratories, and most people's interest has since faded.

But the research process itself gains tremendously by its use of the Internet. Very tough problems that require tremendous calculating power (such as factoring, or breaking down large numbers into parts) can now be split into many smaller pieces to be run on computers scattered around the Net. Amateur scientists, too, can combine their efforts. Backyard astronomers, for example, can coordinate sky surveys for comets or perhaps someday may create a huge network for scanning for messages from alien civilizations.

There is little doubt that teaching, learning, and research are changing as the use of the Internet grows. The shape that schools and laboratories of the future take will be greatly influenced by this new communications technology.

3

Business on the Net

BY 1995 ABOUT 10,000 American corporations were on the Internet, with an estimated 50 to 100 new companies going on-line each day. The Internet is changing the way business managers and workers do their jobs by making it possible to communicate and to manage information in new ways.

The information economy

It takes more and more information to produce goods and services in today's economy. Consider a company that makes a product such as children's toys. The company will probably have a research department that keeps track of new developments in toy design, engineering, and manufacture. There will be a legal department that has to make sure products do not violate federal or state safety regulations. The marketing department will conduct regular surveys of potential customers (parents and children) to determine which toys are likely to be most popular. And, of course, there will be other departments as well: advertising and public relations, payroll and accounting, shipping, and so on. None of these departments produces goods (toys) directly, but rather they work with information that is essential to the business. By 1975 about half of the workers in economically advanced countries dealt with information production; by 2000 the proportion will be about two-thirds.

Because so much information must be tracked by business, any technology that makes it faster or easier to manage information will be important. Computer hardware, software, and networking are thus themselves among the fastest growing industries.

How the Net is changing business

When desktop computers became widely available, something called the "paperless office" was predicted. All the memos, reports, invoices, and other documents could be created using word processors and spreadsheets and stored on disks instead of being turned into stacks of paper. But the reality was different. Because it was not easy to connect computers together, most information was still printed on paper and passed around in "hard copy" form or on floppy disks.

Gradually, however, a number of networking systems for linking the computers within a company became available. One of the first uses for such networks was replacing paper memos and many phone calls with electronic mail. In the old days, a manager dictated a letter to a secretary, who then typed it. After the manager checked it for errors, the secretary mailed it. This whole process cost about $10 per letter! Today many managers don't have secretaries. They type an e-mail message, click the "Send" button, and it is on its way for a penny or two. The e-mail message will arrive at its destination in a few minutes or hours, not several days as with a letter.

By the mid-1990s, the business world began to realize that the Internet offered many advantages over earlier networks. All Internet users used the same kind of address, so it was easy to send messages anywhere in the world. The Internet also offered powerful new tools for organizing and accessing information: newsgroups, mailing lists, networked databases, and the World Wide Web.

As one example, Sun Microsystems, a major computer company, began to use the World Wide Web as a major management tool. "Webmaster" Carl Meske set up an internal web system (called an "intranet") that the company's sixteen thousand workers could use to retrieve the huge numbers of policies, memos, product announcements, technical documents, and reports created by the organization. Meske reports:

> Now we have about 2,000 web sites inside the company, from personal, to project, to group sites, to functional ones. . . . To communicate, people used to send giant e-mails with these files attached. Instead of all this pushing information [on people], why not do this pulling metaphor where people can go and get the information [they need]? Just send them a message with the URL [web address] on it.[15]

Now each department in the company could have its own website, where it could report developments. People throughout the company would know what information was available and could retrieve it quickly and easily. Internal newsgroups using the Netnews software can serve as discussion forums, where people can ask questions about policies and procedures. Chat, newsgroups, and conferencing software could be used to set up meetings without people having to fly across the country. Today intranets serve the information and communication needs of an increasing number of schools, nonprofit organizations, and scientific laboratories, as well as businesses.

Telecommuting and new work patterns

The Internet is not only changing how people work, but also *where*. Just as some students are taking classes without

A businesswoman telecommutes from home while her baby looks on from a crib. Telecommuting is one of the fastest growing business trends.

going to school, a growing number of workers are working without going to work. Working at home rather than at the office is called "telecommuting." Although 1995 surveys showed only about 1 to 2 percent of American workers telecommuted at least one day a week, it is now one of the fastest growing trends in business.

Not all jobs are suitable for telecommuting. A waiter, for example, has to be physically present in the restaurant. But information workers—people who work with words, numbers, and pictures, such as real estate agents, financial analysts, writers, programmers, artists, and designers—can often work from home. Telecommuting can make it possible for a parent to take care of young children at home while still holding a job. By reducing the number of trips to the office, telecommuting also reduces traffic congestion and air pollution.

Telecommuting does have some disadvantages. Most telecommuters keep in touch with their fellow workers by e-mail, which lacks the full range of human communication in face-to-face contact. Telecommuters may be in danger of losing touch with the face-to-face interaction that often determines assignments and opportunities for promotion. Some managers are afraid that telecommuters will lack the self-discipline to get their work done on time.

Technology that simulates face-to-face meetings is becoming more available, however. MIT computer scientist Michael Dertouzos believes that the video equipment and heavy-duty phone lines for full-blown electronic conferencing will probably be too expensive for people to have at home, but he asks us to imagine

> a building, full of good equipment, connected to the rest of the world by high-speed lines. You lease space in this work center, which could be, say, by a beautiful lake in New Hampshire. In the morning, drive to your lakeside work center, park your kids in day care there and go to work for people in Tokyo or San Francisco.[16]

Twenty-first-century jobs

Some information workers are going beyond telecommuting to being self-employed. Rather than working for a company, they offer their services as contractors, doing a particular job for an agreed-upon price. Programmers, writers, researchers, and graphic artists can use the Internet both to find customers and to deliver the finished work.

The Internet also offers many opportunities for entrepreneurs—people who take the risk of starting new businesses. Such businesses can offer Internet connections, design custom websites, and do surveys to help other businesses find customers on the Net. Other businesses can use the Net to sell their goods and services.

No walls, no roofs?

By making it possible for two people anywhere to connect and work together, Nicholas Negroponte believes that on the Internet

> bits will be borderless, stored and manipulated with absolutely no respect to geopolitical boundaries. In fact, time zones will probably play a bigger role in our digital future than trade zones. I can imagine some software projects that literally move around the world from east to west on a twenty-four-hour cycle, from person to person or from group to group, one working as the other sleeps. Microsoft will need to add London and Tokyo offices for software development in order to produce on three shifts.[17]

A "cyber café" in London, England, attracts patrons who wish to use the Internet in a café setting.

It is clear that the Net offers great flexibility for both businesses and workers, as well as previously untapped markets for goods and services. But there may be a price to pay for this flexibility. When there are no walls that divide people into different countries and communities, the "roof" of economic security may also be threatened.

Americans tend to take their leadership in the computer industry for granted. After all, the personal computer was invented in the area south of San Francisco that became known as Silicon Valley. Farther north, in Redmond, Washington, Microsoft, led by multibillionaire Bill Gates, sells the leading operating systems and applications for PCs.

In recent years, however, enterprising people from less industrialized countries have challenged this leadership. India is one of the best examples. During the 1980s, thousands of highly skilled Indian computer scientists and programmers came to work in the American software industry. By the 1990s, however, the work itself was starting to go to

India. Increasingly, programmers in cities such as Bangalore are writing and maintaining software for companies such as General Electric, AT&T, IBM, and Motorola. These corporations and many others are taking advantage of the highly motivated workers and relatively low labor costs they have found in India, Asia, and Eastern Europe.

As the Net becomes worldwide, businesses and workers find themselves competing globally. People with good programming, writing, or design skills will continue to find jobs, but it is far from clear who will gain and who will lose in the twenty-first-century information economy.

4

The Electronic Marketplace

AN INCREASING NUMBER of people use the Internet at school and work. But many people access the Net from their computers at home as well. These home users represent a new opportunity for businesses to market their goods and services. As businesses rush to greet consumers on-line, a number of important issues have arisen.

On-line users are seeking protection from scams and unwanted advertising. As they learn how much of their personal information is stored in computer databases, many people, on-line or not, are demanding laws to protect their privacy. Finally, attacks by so-called hackers have shown the vulnerability of systems that control communications, the flow of money, health care, and even power and water.

According to Nielsen Media Research, by the end of 1996, about 2.5 million people had bought something over the Internet. In just one business area, music, there were over 350 different businesses selling CDs on-line. A site called The Internet Mall has seven "virtual floors" on which browsers can find everything from a handcrafted chair to a home mortgage. While the amount of business being done over the Net is still a tiny fraction of that done in stores or by mail or phone orders, experts are predicting a steady increase in "Internet commerce" into the next century.

The respected business magazine *Fortune* notes this development with enthusiasm:

> Remember when companies used to ask "Should we do business on the Internet?" Nowadays, the question is more likely

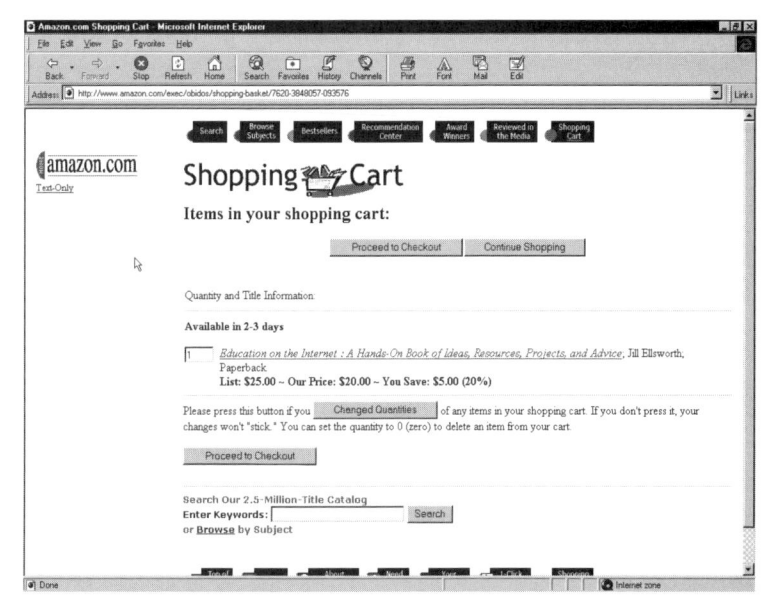

Many kinds of goods and services can be ordered and paid for on-line. Shopping sites collect users' choices in a "shopping cart" where they can be reviewed before final purchase.

to be "How fast can we get going and how can we make it work to better serve our customers and suppliers?" Propelled by the explosive growth of the World Wide Web—which has made network communications inexpensive and virtually ubiquitous [available everywhere]—plus the rapid development of industrial-strength software applications designed for real-life transactions, electronic commerce has moved from being the technology of the future to being today's strategic imperative [necessity].[18]

One of the most successful businesses to operate on the Internet is Amazon.com, an on-line bookstore. An on-line store does not have to rent expensive mall space. Amazon.com offers books at discount prices lower than those of most traditional bookstores, and it has done so well that large chain bookstores such as Barnes and Noble have started their own Internet sales operations.

But on-line stores have advantages other than price. According to Andrew Kantor, editor of a new magazine called *Internet Shopper*,

> The fact is that you can do things on-line that you can't do in person, like offer extensive reader reviews, interactive book-recommendation services, and worldwide reader discussions. As the on-line bookstores fight it out, consumers end up getting great deals and terrific services.[19]

The increasing use of the Net may hurt some businesses, however. For example, local bookstores already face competition from the large chains. One way they have fought back is to offer personal services, such as knowledgeable clerks who can recommend books to a customer. The on-line bookstores, however, can offer both the large stocks and low prices of the chains and information to help buyers make purchases. Of course, it is still not possible to go to an on-line bookstore, pick up a book at random, and browse.

Some local businesses can benefit from using the Net. Restaurants can put their menus on-line and make it easy for people to reserve tables or to order meals to be delivered to their home. In general, service businesses such as restaurants and grocery stores that must be physically present in the neighborhood can use the Net to make their services more attractive and easy to use. But local businesses selling nonperishable merchandise that can be shipped anywhere (such as books and CDs) may find it harder to compete.

Advertising or "spam"?

From the point of view of many businesses, the Net offers a powerful, low-cost way to attract new customers. The very ease of use of this technology has created new problems, however. In 1994 a law firm offering immigration-related services flooded thousands of Usenet newsgroups with announcements offering (for a charge) to obtain and file forms that were actually available from the government for free. Many Net users did not think highly of this offer. What made them even less happy was the fact that the ads were posted in newsgroups that had nothing at all to do with immigration or legal matters. Advertising that is automatically and indiscriminately spread throughout the Net became known as "spam" after a famous *Monty Python* skit about a canned meat product.

Spam is a good example of how the technology of the Net can have unexpected consequences. On the Net, most people do not pay a fee to deliver an e-mail message or to post a news article. In addition, it is easy to write programs to automatically scan newsgroups, mailing lists, and websites and to record thousands of e-mail addresses. Whether one or ten thousand, the cost is the same. A "spammer" need only get a flat-rate account from an Internet service provider, feed the list of addresses to a program, and generate thousands of spam messages.

Spam can sometimes flood Net connections, preventing people from receiving mail they want. If it floods a newsgroup, spam makes it hard for readers to find the articles they want to read. One Internet user, Tom Ritchford, asked people to

> imagine that you are sitting in a café, talking to a few friends. Then, someone comes in with a megaphone and proceeds to deliver an advertisement, in fact an advertisement that is trying to sell for $75 something you can get for free. You later discover that this individual has done this in every café in the city . . . and that this individual intends to do this repeatedly.[20]

Expert Internet users soon began to fight back. They wrote programs called "cancelbots" (cancelation robots) that tracked down spam news messages and tricked the Netnews software into removing them from the newsgroups. Many network service providers also agreed that they would not allow their accounts to be used for spamming. Some providers went further: They began to block mail coming from sites that were used mainly by spammers.

There have been a number of other proposals to control spam. These range from laws to prohibit unsolicited e-mail advertising to an agreement that all advertising mail have a keyword (like "advertisement") in the subject header. In the latter case, mail programs could set up "filters" that would automatically delete advertising if the user did not want it.

Buyer beware

Spam may be rude, but it is more of a nuisance than a threat. A more serious problem is fraud. Since just about anyone can get onto the Internet and open a store, it is hard for consumers to be sure they will not be cheated.

A number of classic cons, or swindles, have found a home on the Net. For example, there are "pyramid schemes," where one person is asked to sign up perhaps ten others, each of which is supposed to sign up ten more, and so on. Since each person who signs up pays a fee, everyone is supposed to eventually receive a large amount of money from people who sign up later. Of course, pyramid schemes soon run out of participants, leaving many people having paid something and received nothing. Pyramid schemes are illegal.

Even if one avoids swindles, ordinary transactions can cause problems. The traditional business world has the Better Business Bureau and government agencies to which a consumer can complain if a product is not received or is defective. Although on-line businesses are subject to commercial laws, it can be very difficult to track down a "store" that can disappear into cyberspace. Consumer experts suggest that people be careful when buying things on the Internet from companies they have never heard of.

If the Net has dangers, it also has solutions. Consumer agencies on-line can rate or certify Internet businesses. Credit card companies can work to protect their users. News and discussion groups can also help consumers sort out the good deals from the bad.

"Hacker" attacks, threats, and responses

Computer systems give great power to people who have a deep understanding of how they work. Like all power, it can be used for good or bad purposes.

Starting in the late 1950s, young computer users at places such as MIT and Caltech became obsessed with the first interactive computer systems. They became known as hackers, and they spent many hours at computer keyboards. They wrote short, elegant programs that added new features to computer systems. They invented computer games. These early hackers saw the computer as a tool with limitless possibilities. According to author Stephen Levy, hackers

> believe that essential lessons can be learned about the systems—about the world—from taking things apart, seeing how they work, and using this knowledge to create new and even more

interesting things. They resent any person, physical barrier, or law that tries to keep them from doing this.[21]

Why do hackers hack? Computer security expert Dorothy Denning interviewed some and noted:

> One insisted that "Hackers understand something basic about computers, and that is that they can be enjoyed. I know none who hack for money, or hack to frighten the company, or hack for anything but fun." Another young hacker remembered that "Hacking was the ultimate cerebral [mental] buzz for me. I would come home from another dull day at school, turn my computer on, and become a member of the hacker elite. It was a whole different world where there were no condescending adults and you were judged only by your talent. . . . To go along with the adrenaline rush was the illicit thrill of doing something illegal. Every step I made could be the one that would bring the authorities crashing down on me. I was on the edge of technology and exploring past it, spelunking into electronic caves where I wasn't supposed to be."[22]

At first, hacking was little known outside the computer laboratories. In the 1980s, however, magazine readers began to learn about young hackers who went by names like

Phiber Optick and Acid Freak. The articles were usually sensational and alarming, warning that hackers could steal thousands of credit cards or even jam the emergency 911 phone system. Fascinated readers followed accounts of epic battles, such as that between hacker Kevin Mitnick and scientific computer wizard Tsutomo Shimomura. Shimomura eventually helped authorities track down Mitnick, who was sentenced to prison for breaking into computers and stealing credit card numbers.

Hacking can affect the whole network, not just a single computer. On the evening of November 2, 1988, Internet users began to notice that more and more systems were slowing down. Eventually six thousand systems crashed, bringing business, government, and scientific institutions to a halt. Computer scientists learned that one of their young colleagues, Robert Tappan Morris Jr., had written a program called a "worm." The program was designed to use a flaw in the e-mail system to travel automatically on the Internet, making more copies of itself wherever it went. Although the worm did not destroy any data, it tied up computer resources and it cost somewhere between $15 million and $100 million to remove all copies of it from the Net.

While the public fear of hackers seems to be exaggerated, there is no doubt that the computers that carry on billions of dollars worth of business every year can indeed be vulnerable. Criminals and spies can steal valuable information from poorly guarded systems. Terrorists may be able to introduce viruses, programs that unlike Morris's worm, can take over computers and make them erase data files.

Protecting privacy and identity

Lawmakers will have to strike a balance between the benefits of free movement of information and the need to protect vital computer systems. Meanwhile, the best line of defense against destructive hackers is knowledge on the part of both system managers and ordinary users. Most hacker break-ins come not through clever programming, but because users assign themselves easy-to-guess passwords, such as their birth date or the name of their favorite musical group.

There is another way to protect valuable information. During the Cold War (1945–1990), governments did much research into encryption, or methods of encoding text so that it could only be read by someone who knew the secret "key"—a special set of characters that could be used mathematically to turn the code message back into readable text. In the United States, the National Security Agency, or NSA, jealously guarded the most effective methods of encryption. But all code systems had a weakness in that the secret key might be intercepted by someone who could then read the messages.

In 1975, however, a computer scientist named Whitfield Diffey devised a new method called "public key cryptography." This system used a complex mathematical formula to generate pairs of keys. The keys in a pair have a special relationship: Text encoded using one of the keys can only be read using the other key. A person can distribute one key in the pair, called the public key. Anyone using the public key can encode a message that can be read only by the person holding the corresponding private key. The private key itself need never be sent anywhere, so no one can steal it.

Further, if one receives a message encoded with a person's private key, one can be sure it was sent by that person. The private key could thus serve as a "digital signature" that verifies the identity of the sender.

The public key system was more secure than earlier systems, but it presented government agencies with a problem. If criminals or terrorists use the system to plan their activities, police would find it almost impossible to decode their messages. The NSA was particularly concerned that foreign countries that might be unfriendly to the United States not gain access to the new technology.

In 1984 cryptographer and political activist Phil Zimmermann changed the rules of the game. He created a version of public key cryptography using a program that could run on just about any computer, including popular PCs. In a message included with the program he declared:

> If privacy is outlawed, only outlaws will have privacy. Intelligence agencies have access to good cryptographic technology. So do the big arms and drug traffickers. . . . But ordinary people and grass-roots political organizations mostly have not had access to affordable military-grade public-key cryptographic technology. Until now.[23]

Security experts such as Dorothy Denning warned that freely available encryption could seriously hurt law enforcement:

> If we fail to pass legislation that will ensure a continued capability for court-ordered surveillance, systems fielded without an adequate provision for court-ordered intercepts would become sanctuaries for criminality wherein Organized Crime leaders, drug dealers, terrorists, and other criminals could act with impunity. Eventually, we could find ourselves with an increase in major crimes against society, a greatly diminished capacity to fight them, and no timely solution.[24]

Law enforcement leaders including Louis Freeh, head of the FBI, proposed that a standard device called the Clipper chip be used to provide encryption. The Clipper chip would be easy to use, but it would have a "back door" that would allow law enforcement agents to read messages without the key. Advocates assured the public that this would only be done after obtaining a court order similar to a search warrant. An alternative proposal did not use a Clipper chip. It simply required that users of any form of encryption deposit a copy of their key with a government agency. Upon receiving a court order, the agency would release the key to law enforcement officials.

Meanwhile, the federal government banned the export of encryption software, using laws that normally apply to weapons of war. Zimmermann was threatened with prosecution for distributing his PGP (Pretty Good Privacy) software on the Net.

But in late 1997 Congress seemed to be moving the other way when the House Commerce Committee voted to end export restrictions on encryption software and refused to require that any user of encryption deposit a copy of his or her private key with a government agency. Meanwhile, a federal court in San Francisco ruled that software, like writing, carried ideas and was a form of free speech protected by the First Amendment to the Constitution.

Although the legal issues have not all been settled, practically speaking, it would be very hard to stop people from using software such as PGP on the Net. "Cracking" such codes, if possible, requires very powerful computers. Tracing e-mail messages can be very difficult because the electronic return addresses can be forged or even made anonymous.

Electronic cash

Encryption can protect privacy. It can also make the electronic marketplace more secure for both businesses and consumers.

Electronic systems have played a major part in banking and commerce for many years. Credit cards became widespread in the 1960s and were followed by automatic tellers in the 1980s. In the mid-1990s, as businesses set up shop on the Internet, they needed to provide a way that consumers could order their purchases and pay for them.

At first, some on-line merchants put a catalog on-line, but required that customers call an 800 number or use a fax to send their order and credit card information. Some

The Electronic Frontier Foundation is an organization that advocates free speech and protection of privacy on the Internet.

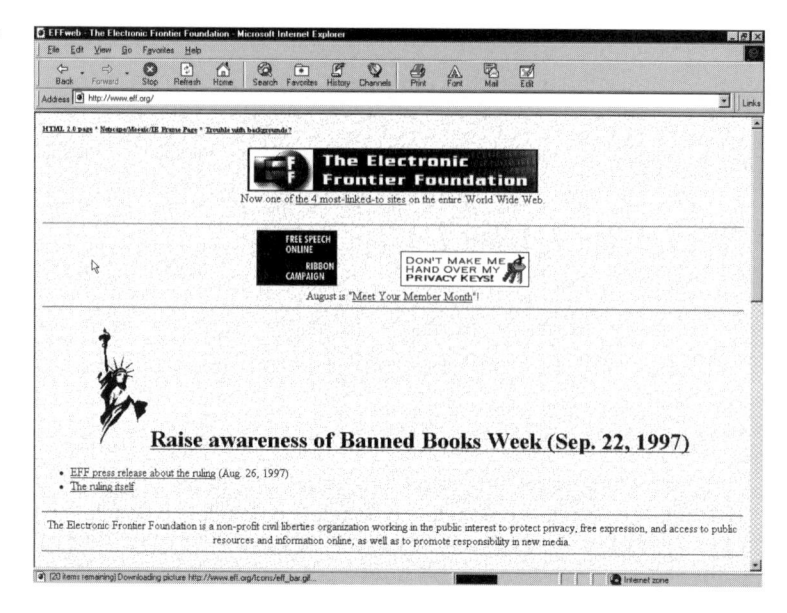

stores accepted orders by e-mail, but experts warned that ordinary e-mail could be easily read by hackers who had broken into a system or even intercepted as it moves through the network.

In response, Internet server and browser developers introduced systems that could take an on-line order form filled out by the consumer and automatically encrypt it before sending it to the merchant. These "secure transaction systems" make it unlikely that credit card numbers can be stolen on-line.

Credit cards have some drawbacks, however. Only merchants large enough to afford the transaction fees can accept them. The fees also make it unprofitable to use credit cards for small transactions, such as an author charging on-line readers fifty cents to read a short story. Several systems are now being developed that offer "electronic currency." To create electronic currency, a company uses special coded messages that give the owner the right to a certain amount of cash that is being held on deposit—much like a dollar bill once represented a certain amount of silver deposited in the U.S. Treasury.

A consumer can buy electronic currency from an on-line bank and use it to buy goods and services from merchants.

The merchant's software verifies that the currency is authentic and sends it to the on-line bank, which credits the proper account.

Because it is so highly automated, electronic currency might be inexpensive to use even for small transactions. Electronic currency is also more private than credit cards, since no permanent record is kept after it is used. Because of this, government officials are concerned that electronic currency can be used by criminals to deal in illegal goods such as drugs or simply to avoid having to pay sales taxes.

The larger debate

As with many other issues, on-line privacy becomes part of a larger debate in our society about how much privacy individuals should have in their daily activities. Today computers store huge amounts of information about one's buying habits, credit record, and even health. Websites even create small files called "cookies" that record information about a user's browsing habits, preferences, or identity.

The information gathered by businesses and other institutions can help them tailor their services to individual needs. Being able to target certain kinds of customers can make advertising more effective and reduce costs. On the other hand, insurance companies can use health records to decide not to insure people who they find have certain medical conditions that are likely to be costly. Incorrect credit information can prevent a person from being able to buy a house or even affect the chances of getting a job.

Much information stored by credit agencies is not very secure. Hackers have demonstrated that they can go on-line and obtain a great deal of information about a person. Such information can be used to impersonate people, order goods with their credit cards, and even to apply for new cards in their name.

By making it easier to both store and obtain information about people, the Internet is forcing lawmakers and consumers to make difficult decisions about what information may be gathered and to whom it can be distributed.

5

Information in the On-Line Age

FOR THE BUSINESSPERSON, information is mainly a tool to be used to create and sell products. For some professions, however, information is not something that helps produce things—it is the product itself. As the way information is gathered, organized, and delivered changes, professions such as library science and journalism are having to change as well.

Plugged-in librarians

Librarians have traditionally had the important job of collecting and organizing information and of helping people find the information they need. The information has generally been in the form of books, magazines, and newspapers, although in recent years sound recordings and videos have become more important.

From the 1980s on, many libraries converted their card catalogs into on-line catalogs that library users could use to quickly and easily find materials by author, subject, title words, and so on. Meanwhile, new technology made it possible to store encyclopedias and collections of documents and images on discs called CD-ROMs. Web browsers can be set up to present material from a disc in the same way pages from the Internet are shown.

Computer magazines began to feature articles of a "library of the future" where all the books and magazines in the world would also be on discs or would be available

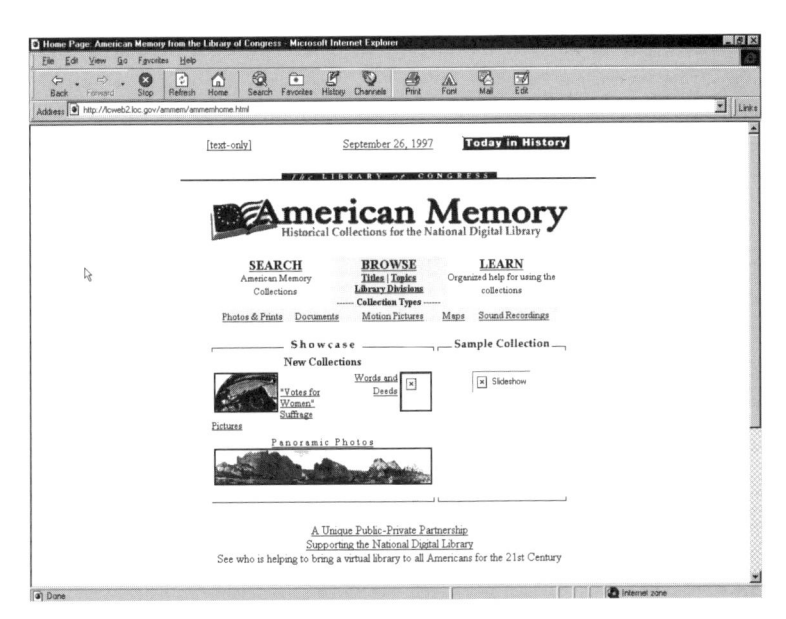

American Memory is a site that gathers original historical documents and makes them available to researchers on-line.

from on-line databases. CDs are much more compact than books. But putting the millions of different books in the world on a computer is a difficult task. Just scanning in all the pages of all the books would involve a huge amount of labor. Yet a beginning has been made. Two projects, the On-line Book Initiative and Project Gutenberg, are assembling libraries of books that have been turned into electronic form. Project Gutenberg hopes to have ten thousand books available for a *total* cost of about $100 on compact discs. This means that a school, or even a single classroom, can have a library as large as the entire public library of a small town. The Library of Congress is also putting many historical documents on-line.

A need for "info-navigators"

Someday library buildings filled with books may disappear, and everyone will be able to find and read any book using a handheld computer. But this does not mean that librarians will no longer be needed. The bigger the Net and the World Wide Web become, the harder it may become to know how to find particular information or to decide which information is reliable. MIT computer scientist Michael Dertouzos believes that "there will be a tremendous amount of info-junk [on the Net] and we're going to need intermediaries to sort through it. We will need info-tailors, info-brokers, info-navigators."[25] These workers may be part reference librarian and part entrepreneur.

New forms of media

The day the whole Library of Congress is on a computer may be far off, but more and more magazines and newspapers are creating electronic editions in the form of websites. The on-line version of a newspaper can contain additional stories and background material that will not fit into the amount of space available in the printed edition. It can have classified ads with a convenient search feature. News stories can be updated continuously on-line. This can give some of the "live" quality of television or radio together with the depth of detail provided by the printed word. The on-line newspaper can also be marketed to people who live too far away to have the print edition delivered.

Traditionally, if a newspaper reader has a comment about something in the paper, he or she writes a letter to the editor. But the on-line newspaper can be much more interactive. A chat or conference feature can be added so readers can discuss the stories they have just read.

The Internet has blurred many of the distinctions between different forms of media. A talk radio show or a TV soap opera can have a website. Many big Hollywood movies now have their own websites set up by the studio to publicize the film. And while traditional media branch out onto the Internet, Microsoft and other big computer companies seem to be expanding into television and movies. For example, Microsoft has joined NBC to form a new television network, MSNBC.

While many forms of media are taking advantage of the Internet, the Net may be borrowing an idea from TV. Most web users eventually have several favorite sites that they rely on for news about topics that interest them. But it is tedious to have to navigate to each of these sites every day to see if any new material has been posted. It would be like

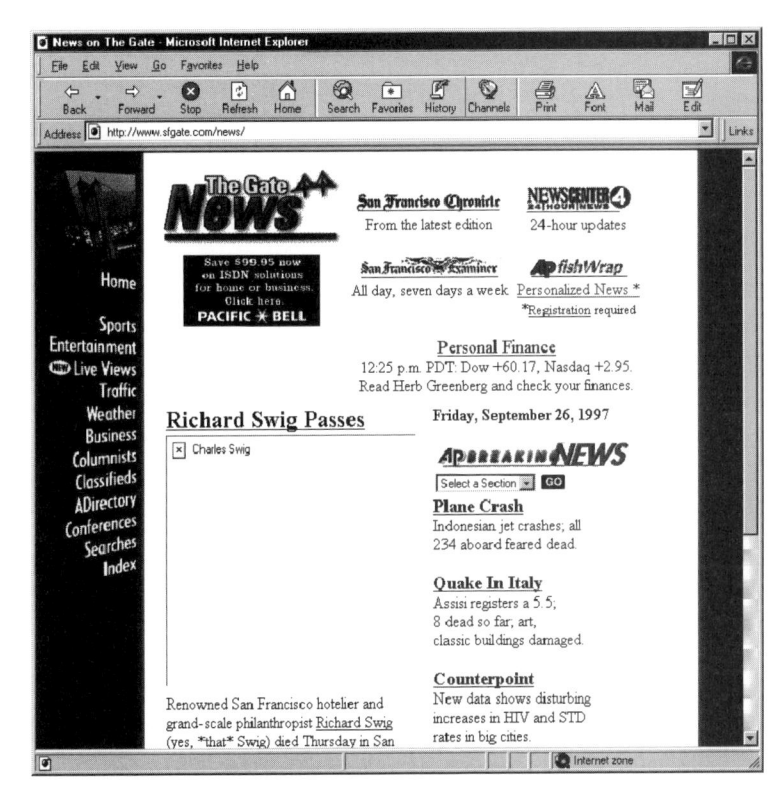

Many newspapers and magazines now have electronic editions available on the World Wide Web.

having to search the news wires for stories every day instead of receiving a morning newspaper.

The major Internet browsers are now offering a way to sign up to receive a continuous supply of news and other information from the Net. Just as there are many TV channels offering a variety of different kinds of programming, "webcasting" (also called "push" technology) groups a number of participating sites into "channels" that the user can choose to receive. For example, a user can choose a sports channel and receive a continuous update of how his or her favorite team is doing.

Perhaps the ultimate marriage of Internet and TV is called WebTV—a TV set that includes a box that connects it to the Internet as well as the regular cable TV service. The WebTV user can watch regular TV shows or, with the flick of a switch, start browsing websites. Because it lacks a regular computer keyboard, however, WebTV is rather awkward to use for extensive web browsing.

Ultimately, intelligent software "agents" may observe users' on-line choices and ask questions about preferences. Using this information, the agent could sift through the Net looking for the kinds of information a person most likely wants to see, even suiting it to the time of day.

Looking toward the future, media pioneer Nicholas Negroponte asks us to imagine:

> What if a newspaper company were willing to put its entire staff at your beck and call for one edition? It would mix headline news with "less important" stories relating to acquaintances, people you will see tomorrow, and places you are about to go to or have just come from. In fact, under these conditions, you might be willing to pay the *Boston Globe* a lot more for ten pages than for a hundred pages, if you could be confident that it was delivering you the right subset of information. You would consume every bit (so to speak). Call it *The Daily Me.*
>
> On Sunday afternoon, however, we may wish to experience the news with much more serendipity [random luck], learning about things we never knew we were interested in, being challenged by a crossword puzzle, having a good laugh with Art Buchwald [a humorous columnist], and finding bargains in the ads. This is *The Daily Us.*[26]

Electronic journalism

But what is happening to the people who must find and report the news in the age of the Internet? As newspapers, magazines, radio, TV, and the Internet seem to be coming together into a huge mosaic of information and entertainment, distinguishing trustworthy from unreliable information may become increasingly difficult. Educational technology expert Don Blake believes that "the most difficult challenge for the next generation will not be gaining access to information, but deciphering and discriminating among it—in other words, being 'information-literate.'"[27]

Traditionally, even highly educated people relied on only a few sources of news, such as CNN, the *New York Times*, a local newspaper, and perhaps a few magazines. Each of these organizations has a stake in its reputation for reliability and integrity. Recognizing this, most people will believe that a story in the *New York Times* is factual but will

Increasing numbers of executives are using the Internet at home to decrease time spent away from their families.

not believe that a story in a supermarket tabloid newspaper is likely to be true.

One of the biggest strengths of the Internet is that anyone who can afford a computer and a phone line can become his or her own reporter, editor, and news service. Now almost anyone can have a "printing press" and freedom of speech. This means that the Internet has a much wider variety of opinions than most newspapers.

On the other hand, unless an Internet user recognizes that a site belongs to a reputable news organization, there is no way of knowing who stands behind a particular story. Rumors can travel through the Internet like wildfire. In 1994, for example, many users panicked when they received warnings about a "Good Times" computer virus. This program was supposedly found in certain e-mail messages. Just reading the message could, it was claimed, destroy data on the user's system. The virus did not exist.

The Internet challenges users to become good critical thinkers. In a way, users must become their own journalists—seeking more than one source for a story, comparing different accounts, and remembering to apply a bit of skepticism.

Who owns information?

For writers and publishers, information is a product that can be sold. The U. S. Constitution gives the federal government the power to grant copyrights to writers. Without copyrights, a person who writes a popular novel or how-to book would not be able to prevent someone else from copying the book, selling it, and keeping the profit.

In the past, copyright protection has usually been effective. Printing actual books is expensive, and books are physical objects that can be seized if they are made illegally. But on the worldwide network, ideas are streams of electronic bytes that can come from anywhere and go everywhere. Indeed, with a scanner, a magazine article or even a whole book can be turned into electronic text and distributed without the consent of the author or publisher.

As Internet intellectual freedom activist John Perry Barlow points out:

> When [Thomas] Jefferson and his fellow creatures of the Enlightenment designed the system that became American copyright law, their primary objective was assuring the widespread distribution of thought, not profit. Profit was the fuel that would carry ideas into the libraries and minds of their new republic. Libraries would purchase books, thus rewarding authors for their work in assembling ideas . . . but what is the role of libraries if there are no books? How does society now pay for the distribution of ideas if not by charging for the ideas themselves?[28]

Electronic text can be protected by encryption—turning the words into gibberish that can only be interpreted by someone who has the proper key or password. But perhaps the best way to protect information is to make it not free, but inexpensive. Once systems are set up that let users read information they want to see for a few pennies a page, there may be little incentive to distribute it illegally.

6

Virtual Communities

THE INTERNET IS changing the way people learn, work, and buy things. The Net's greatest impact, however, may be on how people relate to one another. Shortly after users began to post messages on the early computer networks, they began to have what one might call "out-of body-experiences." For example, in the early 1970s, according to Katie Hafner and Matthew Lyon,

> two people had logged in to the University of Utah [computer system]. One saw that somebody else he knew but had never met was logged in. They were in talk mode, so he typed, "Where are you?" The other replied, "Well, I'm in Washington." "Where in Washington?" "At the Hilton." "Well, I'm at the Hilton, too." The two turned out to be only a few feet from each other, attending the same conference.[29]

When people are on-line, their actual physical location does not matter. In 1984 science fiction writer William Gibson's novel *Neuromancer* coined the term "cyberspace" to describe the imaginary place that people create in their minds as they interact with computer networks. Whether "chatting" one on one, participating in ongoing conferences, or playing fantasy characters in detailed game worlds, many Internet users are creating a rich social life on-line.

On-line discussion forums

There are a variety of places where on-line users can meet to have a discussion. In Usenet newsgroups and mailing lists, a user reads the available messages and possibly replies to a message or posts a new one. The user then returns hours or days later to read whatever new material has accumulated. Discussions can be quite vigorous, but it lacks the rapid interaction of a spoken conversation.

Newsgroups have a rapid "turnover," with postings being automatically removed after a week or so. Another kind of service, called a conferencing system, has long-running discussion topics that can develop over months or even years. One of the oldest and best-known conferencing systems is the WELL ("Whole Earth 'Lectronic Link"), based in the San Francisco Bay Area.

As Howard Rheingold noted in 1987, at the WELL

> there's always another mind there. It's like having the corner bar, complete with old buddies and delightful newcomers and new tools waiting to take home and fresh graffiti and letters, except instead of putting on my coat, shutting down the computer, and walking down to the corner, I just invoke my telecom program and there they are. It's a place.[30]

Users of conferencing systems often develop long-term relationships that extend outside the computer into "real life." Writer Dinty Moore recalls a striking example of this:

> A famous WELL anecdote concerns a young woman, a WELL regular, named Elly who decided to go to the Himalayas and become a Buddhist nun. She was breathing in and out [meditating] for six months or so, had dropped off the WELL, and was almost forgotten, when she suddenly became ill with a dangerous liver ailment. Word was soon posted to the WELL that one of their own was in trouble (Elly had been hospitalized and was in a coma). The WELL regulars, which included doctors, travel agents—one of just about everything—mobilized quickly and efficiently, and arranged for Elly to be flown home.[31]

When a devastating earthquake hit the San Francisco Bay Area in 1989, telephone lines quickly became jammed. But the WELL itself was undamaged, and users dialed patiently until they could get on-line and assure friends that they were all right. The intimacy of the WELL could have negative effects, however. A feud or a failed romance could lead to seemingly endless bickering. The WELL has taken on all the characteristics of a community—a virtual community.

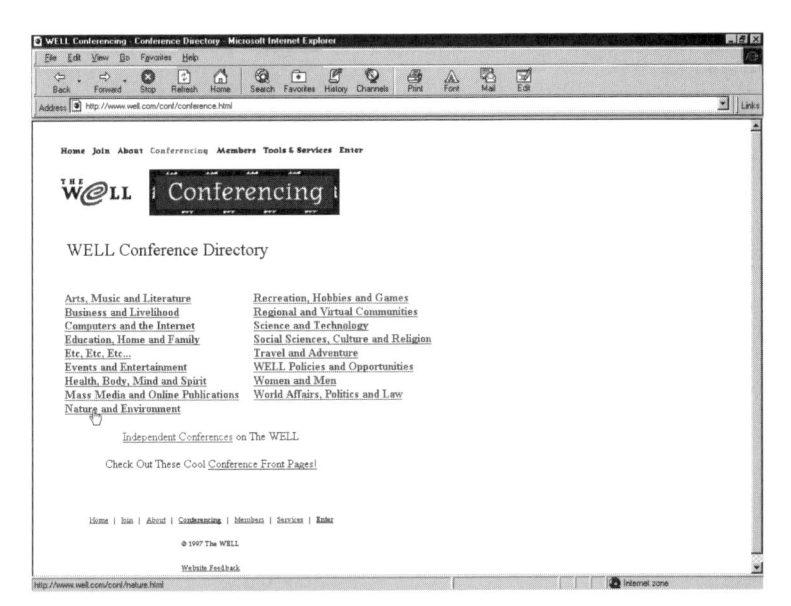

The WELL is one of the oldest conferencing systems. Users can post messages in conferences devoted to topics ranging from politics to pets.

The most direct form of on-line conversation is provided by chat programs, such as those on America Online and on the Internet Relay Chat (IRC) program. With these programs, users sign on to a "chat room" or "channel" devoted to a particular topic. Chat users often assign themselves "handles" or nicknames. Users can address everyone in the "room" at once or send private messages to one or a few other users. Many chat users find this real-time conversation to be exciting and rewarding, but users can also become discouraged by encountering chaotic, unfocused discussions or abusive language.

Shared worlds

Perhaps the most absorbing on-line experience is found in using programs called MUDs, or multi-user dungeons, or similar programs. A MUD is like a chat room, except that it has richly detailed "furniture" in the form of descriptions of objects ranging from a plain wooden chair to a soaring castle.

Unlike a chat user, a MUD user assumes the identity of a fully described character. Depending on how the MUD is set up, the character might represent a fantasy warrior or wizard in a Dungeons and Dragons–style world, the inhabitant of a futuristic city, or even a character in a setting described by psychologist Sherry Turkle as

> an interactive, text-based computer game designed to represent a world inspired by the television series *Star Trek: The Next Generation* [where] thousands of players spend up to eighty hours a week participating in intergalactic exploration and wars. Through typed descriptions and typed commands, they create characters who have casual and romantic sexual encounters, hold jobs and collect paychecks, attend rituals and celebrations, fall in love and get married.[32]

A MUD user builds his or her character by entering commands like the following:

```
@desc me = a tall red-haired Viking
warrior.
```

When another player types:

```
look Eric
```

he or she will see

```
Eric is a tall red-haired Viking warrior.
```

MUD users can also "find" objects, such as weapons and armor. More advanced users can create new objects and add them to the game. The most privileged users, called "wizards," can reshape the game world itself. Some MUD-like programs are not games at all, but imaginative settings for education or conferencing.

The electronic masquerade

The ability to interact with other people in shared worlds can be addictive. Dinty Moore recalls how he was introduced to an Internet user by the following e-mail message:

> Subject: I AM ADDICTED!! HELP!!
>
> My name is Robert and I am totally addicted to "Cyberspace." I was first introduced to the Internet by a friend. At the time I was only MUSHing [playing a computer game]. . . . I did that for the next seven months. I spent the entire day, save breakfast, lunch, and dinner, on the computer. Anything I could do by modem, I would try. The semester just ended at the end of April and I was going to quit playing on the computer but, due to my grades, I have to attend summer classes. Now, I'm back to the same.[33]

Besides going on imaginary swashbuckling adventures, many teenage and young adult Internet users are learning to deal with sexual feelings. The Internet offers a relatively safe place for experimentation. Many chat groups are used for flirting or "cybersex." As Dinty Moore describes it:

> Two people sit alone in front of their respective computers, anywhere in the world. They type onto the screen a description of what they might be doing to one another if they were not separated by three thousand miles, marriage, total lack of acquaintance, and the fact one of them is really just a thirteen-year-old boy pretending to be a voluptuous blonde woman of twenty-five.[34]

Because other users cannot know how old one is or what one looks like, it is possible to experiment with different roles or images of oneself. This can include pretending to be of a different gender. Amy Bruckman has studied this kind of playacting on the Net and notes that

> on the television show *Saturday Night Live*, a series of skits concerned a character named Pat, who has no apparent gender.... Gender is so fundamental to human interactions that the idea of a person without gender is absurd. The audience thinks that surely some clue must reveal Pat's gender, but none ever does....

On many MUDs, it is possible to create gender-neutral characters. It is possible not only to meet Pat, but also to be Pat. When I first met an ungendered character, I felt a profound sense of unease. How should I relate to this person?[35]

By pretending to be a man, a female user can avoid the stereotype that many male users have of women not knowing how to use computers and always needing to be helped. When pretending to be female, a male user is likely to be treated with condescension and bombarded with crude propositions and perhaps may learn something about the harassment women face in daily life.

The Internet has often seemed to be a male-dominated world, but this is beginning to change. According to a 1996 survey, about 38 percent of Internet users under nineteen years old are female. Between 1993 and 1996, the percentage of female users of all ages climbed from less than 10 percent to about 30 percent. As more women make their presence felt on the Net, a female user becomes less of a novelty and more of a colleague who demands respect.

Some MUD users have encountered someone named Julia. She is the ultimate in on-line masquerade. She can flirt and exchange witty remarks in a quite convincing way. But Julia is not a woman, or even a man pretending to be a woman. Julia is a program, a "bot" (robot) programmed to pick up conversational "cues" and interact with human users. Encountering Julia makes one reflect on what it really means to be intelligent.

The ability to hide one's true identity can bring freedom, but it can also encourage people to act in a detached, un-

Who Uses the Web?

Percentage of...	1996	1997
Web Users—Men	64%	57%
Web Users—Women	36%	43%

Source: Yahoo Magazine, Ziff-Davis/Roper.

Rising Computer Use

Hours of use per person

Media	1990	1996	2001*
Television	1,470	1,567	1,551
Radio	1,135	1,091	1,072
Home Video	38	49	60
Video Games	12	26	37
On-line Computers	1	16	39

*Projections

Source: Veronis, Suhler & Assoc.

feeling way. Some users of newsgroups and chat systems like to "flame," or make nasty remarks that turn discussions into arguments. Why is flaming so common? Chris Tanski, a fourteen-year-old "Internet guru" and manager of three Net mailing lists, suggests that it's because

> a large percentage of people who use the net are more likely to consider the person they are corresponding with as a machine rather than a person. This explains why flaming takes place; the flamer thinks of every other user as a terminal or computer. That is because people feel protected or shielded by their computer; people know that the person they flame can't get physical with them because of the distance factor.[36]

Flaming may be a symptom that the on-line experience is something short of full human relationships. According to Clifford Stoll:

> Alone behind a computer, a user needn't interact with anyone in the room. Since keyboards can't be shared, social interactions increasingly take place over the wires. In turn, children feel less connection to their neighborhoods. Hardly surprising that a generation of network surfers is becoming adept at navigating the electronic backwaters, while losing touch with the world around them.[37]

Stoll also believes that

> much of what comes across the computer screen is a surrogate [substitute] for experience. It's living through an electronic

extension of the nervous system—many sensations are dulled, a few amplified. Impoverished proxies [stand-ins] take the place of real events. Which is more fun—playing a video game of basketball or playing a game of basketball?[38]

But to use Stoll's example, most people will never have the real-world experience of coaching an NBA team or executing the flawless moves of Michael Jordan. Computer simulations can offer insight into a complex game that one cannot get by watching it on TV. Over the network, people can compete as though they were basketball coaches or team owners. And after sitting at the computer for a few hours, they can get up, go down to the playground, and shoot a few hoops. Clearly the computer can take over too much of a person's life, but it doesn't have to be that way.

Safety or censorship?

While some critics worry about the long-term consequences of on-line life, others are concerned that the Internet may have more immediate dangers, especially for young people. The July 3, 1995, issue of *Time* magazine had a cover showing the face of a child bathed in the eerie glow of a computer screen. Below the face were the words "Cyberporn . . . EXCLUSIVE: a new study shows how

Don Wright *Palm Beach Post*

pervasive [widespread] and wild it really is. Can we protect our kids—and free speech?"

The study, authored by Martin Rimm, a graduate student at Carnegie Mellon University, claimed that the on-line world was filled with sexually explicit chat lines and graphic material. Critics of Rimm's study suggested that it was badly flawed. For example, they noted that Rimm had included stand-alone adult bulletin board systems (or BBS) that were not part of the mainstream of the Internet.

Nevertheless, there is no doubt that there is pornography on the Net—and there are also images of graphic violence and the rantings of extremist hate groups. Responding to these concerns, Congress passed a law called the Communications Decency Act, or CDA, in early 1996. This law required that all Internet providers make sure that no one under eighteen years old could access any material considered to be "indecent."

Civil liberties groups such as the American Civil Liberties Union (ACLU) went to court to block the CDA. One of their objections was technical: The Internet relies on the free flow of data that can come from anywhere and end up anywhere. Attempts to put roadblocks on the Information Superhighway would be very expensive and probably ineffective. According to network pioneer John Gilmore, "The Net interprets censorship as damage and routes around it."[39]

The other main problem was in the definition of "indecent." According to Supreme Court decisions, each community can set its own standards about what kind of material might be indecent. The standards in a rural town in Georgia are likely to be much stricter than those in San Francisco or Stockholm, Sweden. But because the Net is a global system, an attempt to enforce Georgia's standards might well deprive citizens in San Francisco of material they want to see. Critics argued that the new law would

Demonstrators outside the U.S. Supreme Court in Washington, D.C., protest the availability of pornography on the Internet.

restrict the whole Net to material suitable for children—something like all theaters having to show only G-rated movies because young people can sneak through the doors.

On June 12, 1996, federal district judge Stewart Dalzell handed down his decision on the ACLU's suit. It came down solidly in favor of freedom of speech. He declared that

> the Internet may fairly be regarded as a never-ending, worldwide conversation. As the most participatory form of mass speech yet developed, the Internet deserves the highest protection from government intrusion. . . .
>
> Just as the strength of the Internet is chaos, so the strength of our liberty depends upon the chaos and cacophony of the unfettered speech the First Amendment protects. For these reasons, I without hesitation hold that the CDA is unconstitutional on its face.[40]

In July 1997 the U.S. Supreme Court upheld this decision. The Court said that among other problems, the standard of "indecency" was too vague for people to be able to determine what material was acceptable.

Software solutions

The courts may also have been influenced by the fact that other ways to control objectionable material were becoming available. As with many other aspects of the Internet, many experts believe that technology and the free market may pro-

A four-year-old child plays on a home computer. Laws that would force all material on the Net to be suitable for children have prompted criticism, as has the content of some information on the Internet.

vide a more effective solution than legislation. Parents can now install software programs with names such as CyberPatrol, SurfWatch, or NetNanny. Such programs use two basic methods to keep children from seeing inappropriate material on the Internet. The more restrictive method uses a list of approved Internet sites that is regularly and automatically downloaded and updated. If an Internet address isn't on the approved list, the browser won't show it. The drawback of this method is that it usually blocks a whole site even if only part of it is objectionable. Also, the user must depend on the software manufacturer to keep the list up-to-date, which is difficult given the explosive growth of the Internet.

The other method checks a list of keywords before it allows a site to be displayed. If a word such as "sexy" or "smut" or a racial epithet is found in the site or page name, the site is blocked. The problem with this method is that it does not look at the context, or setting, in which the word is used. For example, it might block a site that deals with safe sex education once it finds the word "sex" or refuse to show a site devoted to breast cancer research because it finds "breast."

It is likely that more sophisticated software will be developed to solve some of these problems. But software guards may not be a substitute for parental involvement. For best results, parents should take the time to use the Internet with their children, become familiar with what is out there, and discuss the rules they expect to be followed.

The politics of information

While politicians and lawyers struggled over the future of the Internet, Internet users were starting to become involved in politics. Because of its low cost and worldwide reach, many political activists have embraced the Internet. According to Howard Rheingold, a pioneer in the area of virtual communities, the Internet may help restore the foundations of democracy:

> If a government is to rule according to the consent of the governed, the effectiveness of that government is heavily influenced by how much the governed know about the issues that

> affect them. The mass-media-dominated public sphere today is where the governed now get knowledge; the problem is that commercial mass media, led by broadcast television, have polluted with barrages of flashy, phony, often violent imagery a public sphere that once included a large component of reading, writing, and rational discourse.
>
> . . . The political significance of [the Internet] lies in its capacity to challenge the existing political hierarchy's monopoly on powerful communications media, and perhaps revitalize citizen-based democracy.[41]

An early example of "electronic democracy" came during the 1980s when electronic activist Dave Hughes found that

> the city planners of Colorado Springs decided to tighten the ordinance that regulates working out of the home. I was the only person to stand up in front of the planning commission and testify against the ordinance; the planners tabled the matter for thirty days. I then brought the text of the ordinance home with me and put it on my BBS.[42]

Hughes then wrote to two local newspapers, giving the phone number for the BBS. Within ten days, 250 people had dialed up the BBS and read the ordinance. In turn, many of them downloaded, printed, and distributed copies of the ordinance throughout the city. At the next city council meeting, more than 175 people showed up to protest the law. As Hughes noted, "Ordinarily, the effort needed to get involved with local politics is enormous. But the economy of effort that computers provided made it possible for me to mobilize opinion."[43]

Internet activism soon became an international phenomenon. In 1989 Chinese dissidents bypassed government censorship and used the Net to tell journalists about the massacre of peaceful demonstrators in Tiananmen Square. In 1991 computer hackers in Moscow relayed blow-by-blow reports on the attempt of hard-line communists to overthrow Russia's infant democracy. A few years later, even the Zapatista rebels of Mexico, though among the poorest of the poor, had their own web page. With all of its shortcomings and despite the fact that many people still have no access, the Internet is increasingly being woven into the fabric of our public life.

Epilogue

A Challenging Future

COMPUTER AND NETWORKING technology seem to be rocketing toward an unimaginable future. While predicting the development of new technology is always difficult, there are several trends that are likely to continue.

Growth in capacity and number of users

Media researcher Nicholas Negroponte points out that

> we are close to being able to deliver 1,000 billion bits per second. This means that a fiber the size of a human hair can deliver every issue ever made of the *Wall Street Journal* in less than one second. Transmitting data at that speed, a fiber can deliver a million channels of television concurrently [at the same time].[44]

The Internet has sometimes suffered growing pains. New services that rely heavily on large graphics and sound files require faster modems, high-capacity phone lines (such as ISDN), and perhaps alternatives to using phone lines, such as including Internet with TV cable service. The number of users and the amount of data delivered are increasing steadily, though.

"Digital convergence"

Negroponte also comments, "I can see no reason for anyone to work in the analog domain anymore—sound, film, video. . . . *All* transmission will be digital."[45] This means that different media, such as sound recording, photography, video, will all be handled digitally, as computer data files. This brings tremendous flexibility and creative opportunity for composers, photographers, and filmmakers. But this flexibility leads to complications. With digital imagery replacing traditional photography, it may soon become impossible to tell whether a picture actually represents reality. This is because a digital photograph of a real person or thing can be altered so that it shows something that never existed. (For example, the creators of the movie *Forrest Gump* inserted the title character into historical footage showing President John F. Kennedy.) The line between news and fiction may become blurred. The journalist, the historian, and even the juror may be unable to make reliable judgments.

Development of virtual communities

As early as 1968, ARPAnet designers J. C. R. Licklider and Robert Taylor asked:

> What will on-line interactive communities be like? In most fields they will consist of geographically separated members, sometimes grouped in small clusters and sometimes working individually. They will be communities not of common location but of common interest.[46]

At the same time that virtual communities bring people together in new ways, they may also isolate people from their neighbors. As Howard Rheingold points out, the on-line world is a kaleidoscope of shifting perspectives:

The Internet's growth has fostered the development of faster modems, high-capacity phone lines, and alternatives to phone service providers, such as cable modem providers.

> Clearly people in the Parenting conference are enmeshed in a social interaction different from that of people in Experts on the WELL, and a college student indulging in the on-line role-playing games known as Multi-User Dungeons lives in a different virtual society from a participant in a scholarly mailing list. Point of view, along with identity, is one of the great variables in cyberspace. Different people in cyberspace look at their virtual communities through differently shaped keyholes.[47]

With all these new opportunities for social interaction, Internet users will be challenged to strike a balance between the on-line world and the local community, where people must work together to deal with problems such as crime, transportation, and the environment.

The future is bringing great challenges and great opportunities. The new tools of on-line communication may help people master the future even as they change it. Perhaps today's young people will be able to bring the worlds within and outside the computer together into a satisfying reality.

Notes

Chapter 1: What Is the Internet?

1. Quoted in Howard Rheingold, *The Virtual Community: Homesteading on the Electronic Frontier*. Reading, MA: Addison-Wesley, 1993, p. 75.

2. Katie Hafner and Matthew Lyon, *Where Wizards Stay Up Late: The Origins of the Internet*. New York: Simon and Schuster, 1996, p. 227.

Chapter 2: The World Is Your Classroom

3. Quoted in Janet Murray, "Schoolkids and the Net," in Philip Baczewski et al., *The Internet Unleashed*. Indianapolis: Sams Publishing, 1995, p. 877.

4. Quoted in Deneen Frazier with Dr. Barbara Kurshan and Dr. Sara Armstrong, *Internet for Kids*. San Francisco: Sybex, 1995, p. 217.

5. Computer Professionals for Social Responsibility, *Serving the Community: A Public Interest Vision of the National Information Infrastructure*, October 1993, p. 11.

6. Quoted in Matt Carlson, *Childproof Internet: A Parent's Guide to Safe and Secure Online Access*. New York: MIS Press, 1996, p. 14.

7. Quoted in "The Web Report Card," *Yahoo! Internet World*, September 1997, p. 56.

8. Carlson, *Childproof Internet*, p. 5.

9. Quoted in Chuck Melvin, "There Is No Race in Cyberspace," *San Francisco Chronicle*, August 31, 1997, pp. D5–6.

10. Clifford Stoll, *Silicon Snake Oil: Second Thoughts on the Information Highway*. New York: Doubleday, 1995, pp. 131–32.

11. Quoted in Andrea R. Gooden, *Computers in the Classroom: How Teachers and Students Are Using Technology to

Transform Learning. San Francisco: Jossey-Bass and Apple Press, 1996, p. xiv.

12. Quoted in Stoll, *Silicon Snake Oil*, p. 141.

13. Quoted in Lisa Gubernick and Ashlea Ebeling, "I Got My Degree Through E-Mail," *Forbes*, June 16, 1997, p. 84.

14. Quoted in Gubernick and Ebeling, "I Got My Degree Through E-Mail," p. 86.

Chapter 3: Business on the Net

15. Quoted in Ryan Bernard, *The Corporate Intranet: Create and Manage an Internal Web Site for Your Organization.* New York: John Wiley, 1996, p. 137.

16. Quoted in Joshua Levine, "Working the Web," *Forbes*, June 2, 1997, p. 180.

17. Nicholas Negroponte, *Being Digital.* New York: Vintage Books, 1995, p. 228.

Chapter 4: The Electronic Marketplace

18. "The Web Gets Down to Business," *Fortune*, Special Advertising Edition 1997, www.pathfinder.com/offers/ecommerce/ecintro.html.

19. Quoted in "Online Bookstores Beat the Real World: Mecklermedia's Internet Shopper Reveals Why They're Better Than 'Brick and Mortar' Shops." On-line document at www.techmall.com/techdocs/TS970917–15.html.

20. Quoted in Dinty Moore, *The Emperor's Virtual Clothes: The Naked Truth About Internet Culture.* Chapel Hill, NC: Algonquin Books, 1995, p. 115.

21. Stephen Levy, *Hackers: Heroes of the Computer Revolution.* Garden City, NY: Anchor Press/Doubleday, 1984, p. 27.

22. Dorothy Denning, "Concerning Hackers Who Break into Computer Systems," in Peter Ludlow, ed., *High Noon on the Electronic Frontier: Conceptual Issues in Cyberspace.* Cambridge, MA: MIT Press, 1996, p. 145.

23. Quoted in Ludlow, ed., *High Noon on the Electronic Frontier*, p. 191.

24. Quoted in Stephen Levy, "Crypto Rebels," in Ludlow, *High Noon on the Electronic Frontier*, p. 196.

Chapter 5: Information in the On-Line Age

25. Quoted in Joshua Levine, "Working the Web," p. 178.
26. Negroponte, *Being Digital*, pp. 153–54.
27. Quoted in Ben Greenman, "The Net Report Card," *Yahoo! Internet World*, September 1997, p. 58.
28. John Perry Barlow, "Selling Wine Without Bottles: The Economy of Mind on the Global Net," in Ludlow, *High Noon on the Electronic Frontier*, p. 13.

Chapter 6: Virtual Communities

29. Quoted in Hafner and Lyon, *Where Wizards Stay Up Late*, pp. 181–82.
30. Rheingold, *The Virtual Community*, p. 24.
31. Moore, *The Emperor's Virtual Clothes*, pp. 87–88.
32. Sherry Turkle, *Life on the Screen: Identity in the Age of the Internet*. New York: Simon & Schuster, 1995, p. 10.
33. Quoted in Moore, *The Emperor's Virtual Clothes*, p. 47.
34. Moore, *The Emperor's Virtual Clothes*, p. 158.
35. Amy S. Bruckman, "Gender Swapping on the Internet," in Ludlow, *High Noon on the Electronic Frontier*, p. 317.
36. Quoted in Frazier, *Internet for Kids*, p. 228.
37. Stoll, *Silicon Snake Oil*, p. 137.
38. Stoll, *Silicon Snake Oil*, p. 149.
39. Quoted in Rheingold, *The Virtual Community*, p. 7.
40. Quoted in Neil Randall, *The Soul of the Internet: Net Gods, Netizens and the Wiring of the World*. London: International Thomson Computer Press, 1997, p. 280.
41. Rheingold, *The Virtual Community*, pp. 13–14.
42. Quoted in Rheingold, *The Virtual Community*, p. 242.
43. Quoted in Rheingold, *The Virtual Community*, p. 243.

Epilogue: A Challenging Future

44. Negroponte, *Being Digital*, p. 23.
45. Quoted in Steven D. Lubar, *InfoCulture: The Smithsonian Book of Information Age Inventions*. Boston: Houghton Mifflin, 1993, p. 158.
46. Quoted in Rheingold, *The Virtual Community*, p. 24.
47. Rheingold, *The Virtual Community*, p. 63.

Glossary

applet: A small program often used to add features to a web page. When activated by a browser, it is downloaded to the viewer's computer and run from there.

ARPAnet (Advanced Research Projects Agency network), later DARPA (Defense Advanced Research Projects Agency): Government agency that funded the development of the network that later became the Internet.

bandwidth: The amount of information that can be distributed in a given time. If one thinks of "pumping" data like water, bandwidth is the width of the pipe.

browser (or web browser): A software program used to view pages on the World Wide Web and to navigate using hypertext links.

CD (compact disc): A shiny disc, written on and read by laser, that can hold a large amount of data, such as text, sound recordings, and graphics images.

chat program: Software that allows on-line users to carry on a conversation by typing messages back and forth.

conferencing system: A facility that organizes on-line conversations on a variety of topics.

cyberspace: A term coined by science fiction writer William Gibson. It refers to the world that computer users experience and share while on-line.

domain: A category of Internet user as given in an address, such as .com (commercial) or .edu (educational).

download: To transfer information from a larger host computer to a personal computer.

electronic commerce: Use of special software to enable the Internet to process orders for goods and services.

electronic mail (e-mail): A message sent to an individual using a computer network.

encryption: Conversion of text into a coded message that can be read only by someone with the correct key.

entrepreneur: A person who starts and runs his or her own business.

FAQ: "Frequently asked questions." A common form of help file that tries to answer most beginners' questions about a topic.

flame: Heated, argumentative, or insulting language used in e-mail or news postings.

FTP (File Transfer Protocol): A program that can copy a data file from one computer or user to another.

hacker: Originally, someone who was obsessed with learning about computer systems and getting them to do clever things. In recent years, the term has been applied to people who seek to destroy computer systems or steal valuable information from them.

header: The part of a data packet (or a mail or news message) that describes who sent it and its intended recipient.

home page: The main page of a website that serves as an introduction and table of contents.

host computer: A computer system that runs software providing connection to the Internet or that runs programs providing other services.

HTML (Hypertext Markup Language): Special commands added to text files to format them for web browsers, such as to show headings, boldface, hypertext links, and so on.

HTTP (Hypertext Transport Protocol): A set of specifications for how browsers and other programs retrieve information from the World Wide Web.

hypertext: Embedding links in a document that connect to other documents.

Internet: The worldwide connection of computer networks that use a common routing system called TCP/IP.

Internet service provider (ISP): A business that offers a connection to the Internet, usually for a monthly service charge.

intranet: A network that uses Internet software but is restricted to users within a particular organization.

Java: A computer programming language often used to add features to web pages.

log on (or log in): To connect to a computer system, usually by giving an ID and password.

mailing list: A discussion group on a particular topic, in which messages are distributed by electronic mail from a central location.

MUD (multi-user dungeon, or multi-user domain): An electronic message system that sets up a game world where users can create characters and fantasy adventures.

netiquette ("net etiquette"): Voluntary guidelines for good behavior on the Internet.

newsgroup: A collection of messages on a particular topic, distributed using Netnews software.

packet: The basic unit into which data is broken up before transmitting it on the Internet. A mail or news message or a web page may contain many packets.

packet-switching: The system by which packets are routed to their destination and reassembled into complete messages or documents.

pornography: Pictures or descriptions intended mainly to arouse a sexual response.

protocol: A set of specifications that describe how computers in a network will communicate, such as for exchanging electronic mail or news messages.

public-key encryption: System where each user has a set of two related code keys. The public key can be used to send messages that can be read only by the person who has the corresponding private key.

server: A computer that provides a resource to be shared by many users, such as file storage space.

spam: Unwanted advertisements sent by e-mail or posted in newsgroups.

TCP/IP (Transmission Control Protocol/Internet Protocol): The basic method for moving data packets around the Internet.

telecommuting: Working from home using a phone connection to a company's computer system.

Telnet: A software program that can be used to connect to a remote computer in order to run a program available there.

URL (Uniform Resource Locator): The address used to locate a web page, file, image, or other resource on the Internet.

virtual community: A group of people who share a common interest and use a chat or conferencing system for discussion.

virus: A program that can trick a computer system into copying it and spreading it around. A virus can include instructions that slow down the system or even destroy data.

World Wide Web (the Web): A system that connects millions of interlinked web pages containing hypertext, graphics, and other features, accessed over the Internet.

Organizations to Contact

Computer Professionals for Social Responsibility (CPSR)
P.O. Box 717
Palo Alto, CA 94302
e-mail: cpsr@cpsr.org

An organization that seeks to deal with social issues that arise from information technology, such as civil liberties, privacy, workplace concerns, and equal access.

Electronic Frontier Foundation (EFF)
P.O. Box 170190
San Francisco, CA 94117
Internet: www.eff.org

The EFF advocates policies that protect freedom of speech in the electronic media.

International Society for Technology in Education (ISTE)
University of Oregon
1787 Agate St.
Eugene, OR 97403-9005
Internet: isteonline.uoregon.edu

The ISTE provides resources and discussion groups for teachers who want to use computer technology and the Internet in their schools. The organization's website provides links to many other organizations.

The Internet Society
12020 Sunrise Valley Dr., Suite 210
Reston, VA 22091
Internet: www.isoc.org/

The Internet Society provides a variety of information about Internet use and coordinates efforts among government, corporations, and educational institutions to use the Internet in productive ways.

The InterNIC
Internet: rs.internic.net/

The InterNIC is a group of companies that have responsibility for assigning Internet domain addresses, maintaining a directory of users, and publicizing new Internet resources.

The Society for Electronic Access
P.O. Box 7081
New York, NY 10116-7081
Internet: www.panix.com/sea/

An organization that works to bring Internet access to underserved parts of the population.

Suggestions for Further Reading

Deneen Frazier with Dr. Barbara Kurshan and Dr. Sara Armstrong, *Internet for Kids*. San Francisco: Sybex, 1995. A useful introduction and activity book for K–12 students.

Ben Greenman, "The Web Report Card," *Yahoo! Internet Life*, September 1997. Grades schools on their use of the Internet, and offers tips for getting homework help on the Net.

Harry Henderson, *Communications and Broadcasting*. New York: Facts On File, 1997. A many-faceted history of communications. It compares computers and networks with earlier inventions.

Harry Henderson and Lisa Yount, *Twentieth Century Science*. San Diego: Lucent Books, 1997. This book has a chapter that looks at the development of computers, multimedia, and artificial intelligence.

Carol Holzberg, "Worldwide Encounters," *Internet World*, September 1996. Describes how students can learn by chatting on-line with their counterparts around the world. Includes a list of sites for K–12 educational resources.

Internet World. While there are now dozens of magazines dealing with various aspects of the Internet and the World Wide Web, *Internet World* is perhaps the oldest and most comprehensive. For subscription information, write to P.O. Box 713, Mt. Morris, IL 61054-0713, send e-mail to iwsubs@kable.com, or check out the website at www.internetworld.com.

Fred E. Jandt and Mary B. Nemnich, *Using the Internet in Your Job Search*. Indianapolis: Jist Works, 1995. A guide to job hunting, résumé writing, and interviewing in the electronic age.

Brendan P. Kehoe, *Zen and the Art of the Internet*. 4th ed. Upper Saddle River, NJ: Prentice-Hall, 1996. One of the best general introductions to using the Internet.

Ed Krol, *The Whole Internet User's Guide & Catalog*. 2nd ed. Sebastapol, CA: O'Reilly & Associates, 1994. Another "classic" and well-written guide to the Internet.

Stephen Levy, *Hackers: Heroes of the Computer Revolution*. Garden City, NY: Anchor Press/Doubleday, 1984. A fascinating and entertaining look at the young programmers who revolutionized the use of computers in the 1950s and 1960s.

Steven D. Lubar, *InfoCulture: The Smithsonian Book of Information Age Inventions*. Boston: Houghton Mifflin, 1993. A well-illustrated account of information-processing inventions from the telegraph to broadcasting to the computer age.

Clifford Stoll, *Silicon Snake Oil: Second Thoughts on the Information Highway*. New York: Doubleday, 1995. A skeptical look at the supposed benefits of computers and the Internet. Delightfully written and thought provoking.

Websites

Alta Vista. One of several "search engines" that indexes keywords and returns a list of matching websites. www.altavista.digital.com/

American Memory. An on-line collection of historical documents developed by the Library of Congress. lcweb2.loc.gov/ammem/ammemhome.html

Kids Web. A site that provides links to help students with class reports on a variety of subjects.
www.npac.syr.edu/textbook/kidsweb

Lycos Top 5% Sites. A site that picks the best websites in each category and rates them.
point.lycos.com/

Yahoo! A subject-oriented guide to recommended Internet sites.
www.yahoo.com/

Additional Works Consulted

Philip Baczewski, et al. *The Internet Unleashed*. Indianapolis: Sams, 1994. A collection of tutorials and essays about using the Internet.

Ryan Bernard, *The Corporate Intranet: Create and Manage an Internal Web for Your Organization*. New York: John Wiley, 1996. A guide to setting up Internet software in a corporate setting.

Matt Carlson, *Childproof Internet: A Parent's Guide to Safe and Secure Online Access*. New York: MIS Press, 1996. For parents who want to learn how to guide and supervise their children's access to the Internet.

Computer Professionals for Social Responsibility, *Serving the Community: A Public Interest Vision of the National Information Infrastructure*, October 1993. A statement of issues and principles involving use of the Internet.

Andrea R. Gooden, *Computers in the Classroom: How Teachers and Students Are Using Technology to Transform Learning*. San Francisco: Jossey-Bass and Apple Press, 1996. Presents examples of how teachers and students have used computers to create new classroom activities and to teach research skills.

Lisa Gubernick and Ashlea Ebeling, "I Got My Degree Through E-Mail," *Forbes*, June 16, 1997.

Katie Hafner and Matthew Lyon, *Where Wizards Stay Up Late: The Origins of the Internet*. New York: Simon and Schuster, 1996. A history of computer networking and the Internet that features remarks by the pioneers who made it happen.

Joshua Levine, "Working the Web," *Forbes*, June 2, 1997. Discusses the Internet from the point of view of the practical businessperson.

Peter Ludlow, ed., *High Noon on the Electronic Frontier: Conceptual Issues in Cyberspace*. Cambridge, MA: MIT Press, 1996. Essays and articles on contemporary issues involving the use and abuse of the Internet.

Dinty W. Moore, *The Emperor's Virtual Clothes: The Naked Truth About Internet Culture*. Chapel Hill, NC: Algonquin Books, 1995. A provocative collection of essays about social interaction on the Net.

Nicholas Negroponte, *Being Digital*. New York: Vintage Books, 1995. Philosophical essays by a digital pioneer and founder of MIT's Media Lab.

Charles Platt, *Anarchy Online*. New York: HarperPrism, 1996. A freewheeling look at the hackers, activists, pirates, and other people who "live" on the fringes of the Internet world.

Neil Randall, *The Soul of the Internet: Net Gods, Netizens and the Wiring of the World*. London: International Thomson Computer Press, 1997. Interviews with the most important pioneers in computer networking and the Internet.

Howard Rheingold, *The Virtual Community: Homesteading on the Electronic Frontier*. Reading, MA: Addison-Wesley, 1993. An introduction to the new electronic communities by a pioneer of the WELL and other conferencing systems.

Sherry Turkle, *Life on the Screen: Identity in the Age of the Internet*. New York: Simon & Schuster, 1995. A psychologist looks at the changing relationship between humans and intelligent machines.

Websites

Basic Information About MUDs. A beginner's guide to on-line fantasy games.
www.assinibionec.mb.ca/user/downes/muds/basic.htm

A Brief History of the Internet and Related Networks, by Vint Cerf. Details of the development of networking by one of its pioneers.
www.simmons.edu/~pomerant/techcomp/cerf.html

Network Wizards. This company compiles a variety of statistics about Internet use.
www.nw.com/zone/

Index

activism, the Net and, 72
address(es). *See under* e-mail; Internet; World Wide Web
Advanced Research Projects Agency. *See* ARPA
Alta Vista (search engine), 19
Amazon.com (on-line bookstore), 43
American Civil Liberties Union (ACLU), 69–70
America Online, 18, 63
ARPA (Advanced Research Projects Agency), 11, 13
ARPAnet, 11, 13

Baran, Paul, 10
Barnes and Noble, 43
BASIC (computer language), 30
batch processing, 12
BBS (bulletin board systems), 69
Berners-Lee, Tim, 14–16
Better Business Bureau, 46
bookmark, 19
bots. *See* robots
browser(s). *See* web browser
bulletin board systems (BBS), 69
business, the Net and, 35–41
  electronic conferencing, 39
  entrepreneurs and, 39–41
  future jobs and, 39
  impact of the Net on, 36–37
  information economy, 35–36
  networking systems, 36
    intranet, 37
  telecommuting, 37–39
  see also electronic marketplace

cancelbots (cancellation robots), 45
catalog site, 18–19
CD-ROM(s), 54–55
censorship, vs. safety, 68–72
Cerf, Vinton, 13
CERN laboratory, 14
chat programs/rooms, 63
Clinton, Bill, 28
Clipper chip, 50–51
commerce. *See* electronic marketplace
Communications Decency Act (CDA), 69–70
communities. *See* virtual communities
computer(s)
  literacy, 30
    defined, 24
  rising use of, 67
Computer Professionals for Social Responsibility (CPSR), 27
conferencing, electronic, 39
  chat programs, 63
  systems, 62
Constitution. *See* U.S. Constitution
cookies (small files), 53
credit agencies, 53
credit cards, the Net and, 51–52
CyberPatrol (software), 71
cyberporn, 68–69
  software solutions to, 70–71
  Supreme Court on decency of, 69–70
cybersex, 65

gender issues/role playing, 65–66
See also cyberporn
cyberspace, origin of term, 61

data packets (datagrams), 13–14
decency, Supreme Court decisions on, 69–70
democracy, electronic, 72
Diffey, Whitfield, 49
digital convergence, 73–74
Digital Equipment company, 12
Distance Learning (guide), 31
distance learning courses, 31–33
DO-IT (Disabilities, Opportunities, Internet-working Technology), 27

education, the Net and, 24–34
  changes in
    age of college students, 32
    learning methods, 25–27
    reference resources, 24–25
    reform, 29–31
    scientists and researchers and, 33–34
    students with Net access, 27–29
    virtual classrooms, 31–32
electronic cash/currency, 51–53
  secure transaction systems and, 52–53
electronic conferencing, 39
electronic democracy, 72
electronic journalism, 58–60
electronic marketplace, 42–53
  advantages/disadvantages of, 42–44
  credit agencies and, 53
  electronic cash/currency, 51–53
  First Amendment issues and, 51
  fraud and, 45–46
  hackers and, 46–48
  privacy and identity and, 48–51
    Clipper chip, 50–51
    encryption, 48–51

  secure transaction systems and, 52–53
  spam(ming) and, 44–45
    cancelbots (cancellation robots) and, 45
  See also business, the Net and; information *entries*
e-mail (electronic mail), 21–23
  addresses, 22
  advantages/disadvantages of, 23
  mailing lists and, 22–23
encryption, 49–55, 60
ENIAC (computer), 10
entrepreneurs, the Net and, 39–41

File Transfer Protocol (FTP), 13
First Amendment, electronic marketplace and, 51
flame/flaming, 65, 67
Fleischmann, Martin, 34
fraud on the Net, 45–46
Freeh, Louis, 50
FTP (File Transfer Protocol), 13

Gates, Bill, 40
gender
  issues and role playing, 65–66
  uses of the Web, 66
Gibson, William, 61
Global SchoolNet Foundation, 25
Good Times (fictitious virus), 59
Gopher (system), 16
Gore, Al, 28

hackers, the Net and, 46–48
Hammer, Randy, 27
handles (nicknames), 63
home page, 16–17
hosts, number of, 7
HTML (Hypertext Markup Language), 16–17
HTTP (Hypertext Transmission Protocol), 15–16
Hughes, Dave, 72

hypertext, 15
  link, 15, 18
Hypertext Markup Language (HTML), 15–17
Hypertext Transmission Protocol (HTTP), 15–16

identity, protection of, 48–51
  Clipper chip, 50–51
  encryption, 49–50
info-navigators, 55–56
information
  economy, the, 35–36
    number of workers in, 35
  electronic journalism, 58–60
  flame/flaming, 65, 67
  intelligent software agents, 58
  libraries, 54–56
  in on-line age, 54–60
    info-navigators and, 55–56
    new forms of media and, 56–58
  ownership of, 60
  politics of, 71–72
    electronic democracy, 72
  rumors and, 59–60
  safety vs. censorship and, 68–72
    Supreme Court on decency, 69–70
  services, 18
  webcasting (push technology), 57
  WebTV, 57
  see also cyberporn
Information Superhighway, 27
intelligent software agents, 58
Internet
  activism on, 72
  addresses described, 19
  digital convergence, 73–74
  e-mail, 21–23
    addresses, 22, 37
    advantages/disadvantages, 23
    mailing list, 22–23
  future of, 73–75
    digital convergence, 73–74
  virtual communities, 74–75
  gaining access to, 17–18
    methods for, 18–20
  history of, 10–16
  home pages, 16–17
  hosts, 22
    number of, 7
  password, 18
  race and, 29
  search engines on, 19–20
  server/service provider (ISP), 18
  surfing, 18–20
  Usenet newsgroups, 20–21
  users
    current number of, 7
    by gender, 66
    ID, 18
    variety of, 16–17
  web browser (program), 18
  see also business, the Net and; education, the Net and; information; and World Wide Web
Internet Mall, 42
Internet Protocol (IP), 13
Internet Relay Chat (IRC), 63
Internet Shopper magazine, 43
intranet, 36

journalism, electronic, 58–60
Julia (robot program), 66

Kahn, Robert, 13
KIDFORUM, 27
KIDLINK, 27

learning methods, the Net and, 25–27
libraries, in on-line age, 54–56
Library of Congress, 55
link(s), 15, 18
  mail, 22

mailing lists, 22–23, 61–63

marketplace. *See* electronic marketplace
media, new forms of, 56–58
  webcasting (push technology), 57
Microsoft, 40
  Internet Explorer (browser), 18
  MSNBC (TV network), 56
minicomputers, 12
Mitnick, Kevin, 48
modem, 18
Morris, Robert T., Jr., 48
Mosaic (program), 16
MSNBC (TV network), 56
MUDs (multi-user dungeons), 63–65, 75
  wizards, 64
MUSHing, 64

NASA, 25–26
National Center for Supercomputing Applications (NCSA), 16
National Security Agency (NSA), 49–50
NBC, 56
NCSA (National Center for Supercomputing Applications), 16
NetDay '96, 28
NetNanny (software), 71
Netnews (programs), 20–21
Netscape Navigator (browser), 18
networking systems and business, 36
  intranet, 36
Network Wizards (company), 6–7
Neuromancer (novel), 61
newsgroups. *See* Usenet newsgroups
New York Times, 58
Nielsen Media Research, 42
NII (National Information Infrastructure), 27

On-line Book Initiative, 55

packet switching, 10–11
paperless office, 36
password, 18
Peterson's college guidebook, 31
PGP (Pretty Good Privacy) software, 51
plug-in utility programs, 16
politics of information, 71–72
  electronic democracy, 72
Pons, G. Stanley, 33–34
privacy, protection of, 48–51
  Clipper chip, 50–51
  encryption, 49–50
  public and private keys, 50–51
Project Gutenberg, 55
public key cryptography, 49–50
push technology (webcasting), 57
pyramid schemes, 45–46

race, the Net and, 29
RAND Corporation, 10
reference resources, on the Net, 24–25
researchers, the Net and, 33–34
Rimm, Martin, 69
robots (bots)
  cancelbots (cancellation robots), 45
  Julia, 66
role playing
  gender issues and, 65–66
  see also MUDs
router, 13
rumors, on the Net, 59–60

safety, vs. censorship, 68–72
SAGE (computer), 10
scientists, the Net and, 33–34
search engines, 19–20
secure transaction systems, 52–53
server, 18
Shimomura, Tsutomo, 48

spam(ming) (unwanted advertising), 44–45
  cancelbots and, 45
start page, 18
Sun Microsystems, 37
surfing the Net, 18–19
SurfWatch (software), 71
system administrator, 13

TCP/IP, 13
telecommuting, 37–39
Time magazine, 68–69
time-sharing operating systems, 12–13
Transmission Control Protocol (TCP), 13

Unix operating system, 14
URL (Uniform Resource Locator), 37
USA Today, 24
U.S. Constitution
  First Amendment, 51
  ownership of information and, 60
  Supreme Court interpretation of decency and, 69–70
U.S. Department of Defense, 11
Usenet newsgroups, 14, 20–21, 61–63
  addresses, 21
user ID, 18

virtual classrooms, 31–32

virtual communities, 61–72
  cybersex, 65
  cyberporn, 68–69
  gender issues/role playing and, 65–66
  development of, 74–75
  MUDs, 63–64
  Usenet news groups and mailing lists, 61–63
virus(es), computer, 48
  Good Times, 59

web browser (program), 18
webcasting (push technology), 57
webmaster, 37
WebTV, 57
WELL (Whole Earth 'Lectronic Link), 62
wizard(s), in MUDs, 64
World Wide Web
  addresses, 15
  described, 19
  URL (Uniform Resource Locator), 37
  history, 14–16
  introduction, 6
  webmaster, 37
  see also Internet
worm (viruslike program), 48

Yahoo! (search engine), 19

Zimmermann, Phil, 50–51

Picture Credits

Cover photo: © Phillippe Plailly/Eurelios/Science Photo Library
AP Photo/Ron Heflin, 33
AP Photo/Patsy Lynch, 69
AP Photo/Steve Rasmussen, 17
AP Photo/Paul Sakuma, 28, 59
AP Photo/Stephan Savoia, 15
Corbis-Bettmann, 12
The San Francisco Gate, 57
© Christopher Smith/Impact Visuals, 70, 74
© Tony Stone Images/Dan Bosler, 38
© Tony Stone Images/Andrew Errington, 40
© 1997, 1998 The WELL, reprinted with permission, 63
© Stacy Walsh Rosenstock/Impact Visuals, 8

About the Author

Harry Henderson has been an Internet user since 1986. He has edited and written books on a variety of computer-related topics, including *Internet How-To* (Corte Madera, CA: Waite Group Press, 1994). He has also written several books on science and technology for young people, including *Twentieth Century Science*, coauthored with his wife, Lisa Yount (San Diego: Lucent Books, 1997), and *Communications and Broadcasting* (New York: Facts On File, 1997). Henderson and Yount work at home in El Cerrito, California, surrounded by five cats, their computers, and an uncountable number of books.

PINE HILL MIDDLE SCHOOL
LIBRARY